D0761977

TE DUE

MARKET SMART

HarperCollins books may be purchased for educational, business, or sales promotional use. For information, please write: Special Markets Department, HarperCollins*Publishers*, 10 East 53rd Street, New York, NY 10022.

First published in 2009 by:
Collins Design
An Imprint of HarperCollins*Publishers*
10 East 53rd Street
New York, NY 10022
Tel: (212) 2s07-7000
Fax: (212) 207-7654
collinsdesign@harpercollins.com
www.harpercollins.com

Distributed throughout the world by:
HarperCollins*Publishers*
10 East 53rd Street
New York, NY 10022
Fax: (212) 207-7654

Interior page design by Anderson Design Group — andersondesigngroup.com
Case histories by Eve Bohakel Lee — editoreve.com
Additional writing by Doug Stern

Cover design by HV ANDERSON DESIGN, Louisville, KY

Library of Congress Control Number: 2008938197

ISBN: 978-0-06-169714-2
Produced by Crescent Hill Books, Louisville, KY
crescenthillbooks.com

Printed in China
First Printing, 2009

MARKET SMART

The Best in Age and Lifestyle-Specific Design

Dr. Daniel Acuff
David Bonner
Jim Gilmartin
Dave Siegel

COLLINS DESIGN
An Imprint of HarperCollins*Publishers*

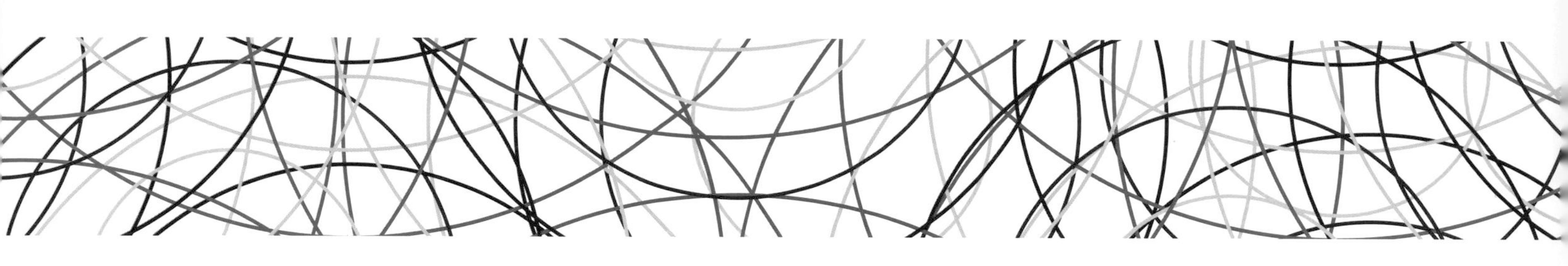

MARKET SMART

CONTENTS

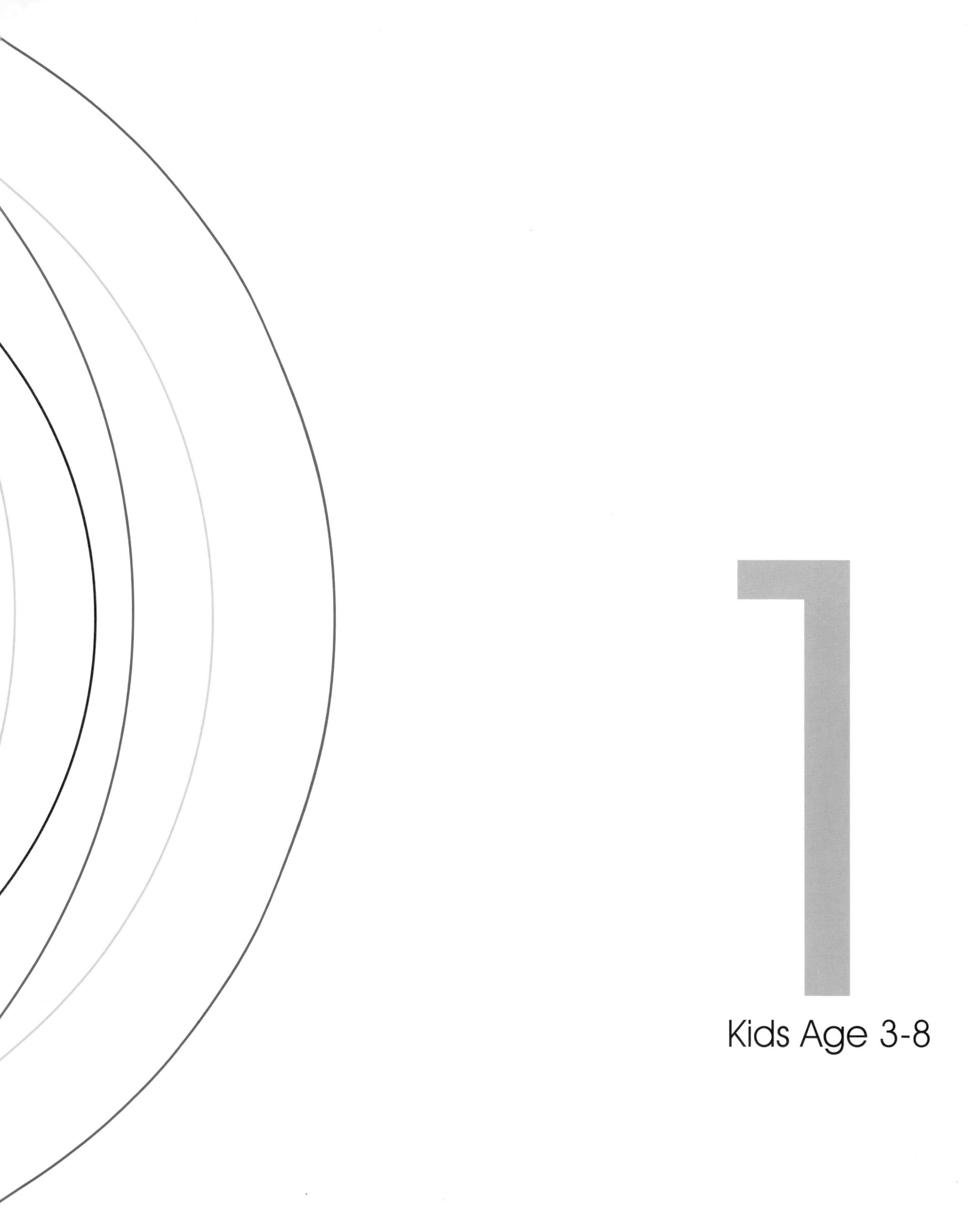

1

Kids Age 3-8

Introduction by Dr. Daniel Acuff

Every project should begin with a clear understanding of the intended consumer.

Most 3- and 4-year-olds do not yet have the ability to read, so verbal information on packaging or other graphics is lost on them. They *do* respond to simpler, larger and brightly colored content without too much edginess.

By the time a child reaches 7 or 8, he now has cognitive abilities that include budding rationality and logical reasoning. He is a more discerning consumer and knows more clearly what he is attracted to and wants—including more edginess.

Bold, high-color graphics with lots of energy are surefire crowd pleasers for young children, and correct use of iconic cartoon characters typically adds greatly to the overall appeal.

While not a step-by-step guide, this model contains components that can serve as a guide when designing for this demographic:

"Bold, high-color graphics with lots of energy are surefire crowd pleasers for young children, and correct use of iconic cartoon characters typically adds greatly to the overall appeal."

Dr. Daniel Acuff is the founder and president of Youth Market Systems Consulting, the Character Lab and coauthor of the books *What Kids Buy and Why: The Psychology of Marketing to Kids* (Free Press, 1998). Dr. Acuff has served as a development, research and marketing consultant to more than 50 major corporations, including Disney, Nickelodeon and M&M Mars, for whom he helped create original characters. He specializes in age segmentation analysis, character creation and development, product and program viability assessment, marketing and advertising. Along with his partner, Dr. Robert Reiher, Dr. Acuff created the YMS system for predicting product viability in the youth market.

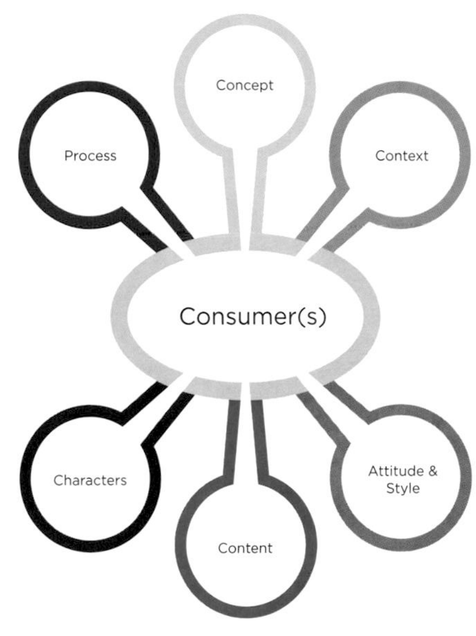

CONCEPT

Concept is the foundation for all creative and execution that follows. The Great Big God CD graphic (page 31), for example, very effectively utilizes a powerful sunburst graphic as a basic design concept.

CONTENT

Content includes both visual and verbal information. The Danimals package (page 13) emphasizes strong and colorful visuals and a monkey character. Even the drinkable yogurt on the package is not static, but splashes up out of its container. Verbal content—in this case, nutritional information—is kept to the bare minimum and included mostly for "mom appeal."

CONTEXT

Context includes both the setting's time period and physical location. Present-day approaches (rather than the past or future) are best for this age range, as are locales or settings such as those featured in the Spider-Man "You're Amazing!" Valentine's Day heart package on page 23.

CHARACTERS

Whether fantasy cartoon characters or real people, characters and kids can be strong attractors. This is utilized quite well on the Sainsbury's Kids packaging on page 20, where the word *kids* visually ties together the concept, content and characters.

ATTITUDE and STYLE

The approach to the graphics may be current, futuristic, anime-influenced, old fashioned, wild or conservative.

PROCESS

The child's reaction to the package may not serve as a simple passive response; the designer may have intended the child consumer not only to view the graphic but also have a particular emotional response to it. Moreover, the package may be designed for the child to open in a special way or continue to use after consuming the contents.

The most attractive graphics for 3- to 8-year-olds are visually dynamic, featuring high-contrast color, bold and fun designs and, often, characters or real kids. Many modern examples throughout the book exemplify the emphasis of the visual over the verbal—an ideal vehicle for appealing to young children.

5 MARKET SMART

One study found that 52 percent of 3-year-olds and 73% of 4-year-olds "often or almost always" asked their parents for specific brands.

When it comes to receiving gifts, kids 6-8 love to get toys more than anything else—more than half (56 percent) prefer traditional toys to electronics and money.[1]

In 2005, advertisers spent $1.4 billion per month (nearly $17 billion) marketing to children—an increase of 15 percent over the previous year, and a 170-fold increase over 1983's $100 million figure.[2]

Kids under 14 spent about $400 billion in 2006, more than six times the $6.1 billion in 1989.[3]

71 percent of kids 9-11 years old stay with a brand or product they like.[4]

84 percent of kids report that they help their parents pick out clothing, 77 percent give input on movies, DVDs and videos to rent, 58 percent have a say in which stores to shop in and half help their parents decide where to go on vacation.[5]

Basic Facts About: Kids Age 3-8

Rules to follow when Marketing to kids age 3-8:

1. **Know your audience!**
   This means understanding your specific targets and how they tick and having a grasp of their cognitive, emotional and social attributes and capabilities.

2. **Understand how young consumers process information.**
   In short, 3- to 4-year-olds grasp information in a more visual, less verbal and logical way than do 6- to 8-year-olds.

3. **Prominently show the product, its features and benefits with the audience in mind.**
   It may be attractive, but is it kid attractive?

4. **Be bold with your visual figures!**
   Make sure they pop—and, in doing so, stand out dramatically from the background.

5. **Have fun!**
   Using humor and excitement will get the audience fired up about your product and that's the emotional impact you seek—and that's more important than cognitive impact.

Design Firm: Zunda Group LLC
Location: South Norwalk, Conn.
Client: The Dannon Company Inc.
Industry: Consumer Package Goods

Design Firm: Design K
Location: Oakland, Calif.
Client: Tattoos For Tots
Industry: Children's Gifts and Toys

Design Firm: Rhythm Visual Communication
Location: Kuala Lumpur, Malaysia
Client: Oriental Food Industries Holdings Berhad
Industry: Confectionery

Design Firm: Prime Studio Inc.
Location: New York, N.Y.
Client: Fiesta Products
Industry: Product Packaging

Design Firm: Executionists Inc.
Location: Marina Del Rey, Calif.
Client: Kidfuel
Industry: Beverages

Design Firm: Pear Design
Location: Chicago, Ill.
Client: Mid-Michigan Children's Musuem
Industry: Children's Museum

hatapillar

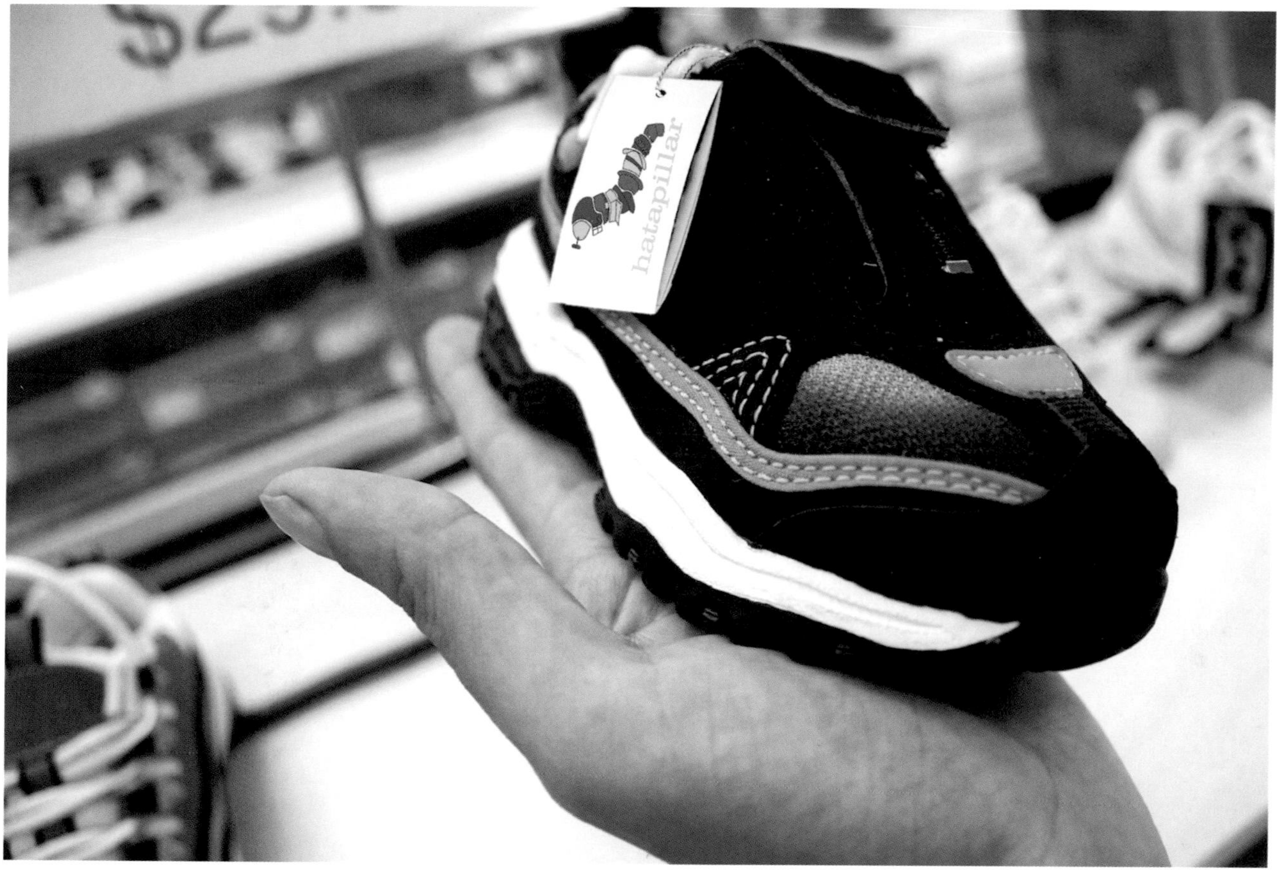

Design Firm: Reactivity Studio
Location: Austin, Texas
Client: Hatapillar Inc.
Industry: Children's Apparel

Design Firm: Euphorianet
Location: Monterrey, N.L., Mexico
Client: Toma Products
Industry: Food & Beverage

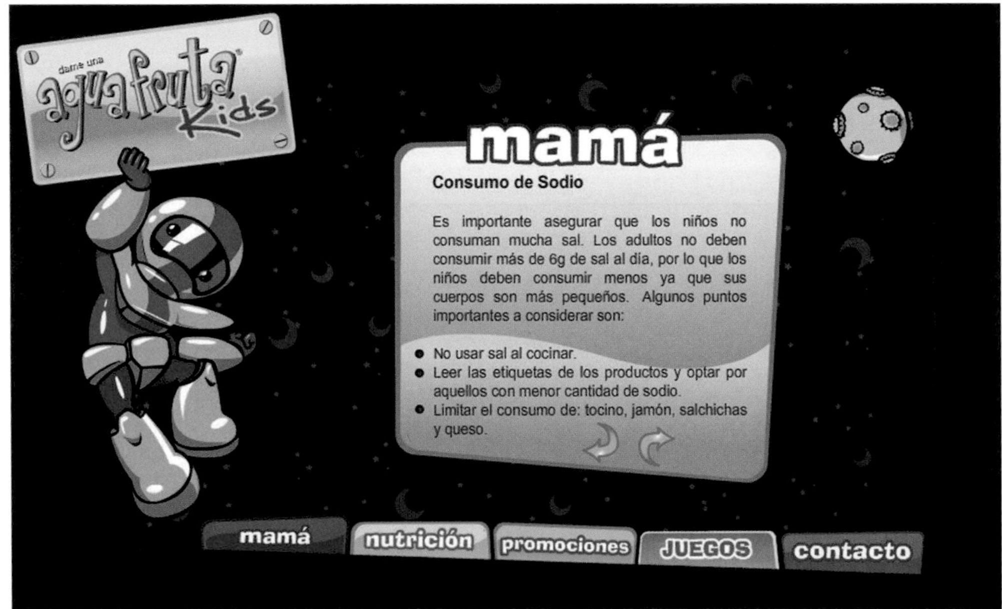

Design Firm: Parker Williams
Location: London, England
Client: Disney
Industry: Toys

Design Firm: Epos Inc.
Location: Hermosa Beach, Calif.
Client: Los Angeles Public Library
Industry: Public Library

Sainsbury's Kids

When the mid-market U.K.-based supermarket chain Sainsbury's decided to create a kid-friendly food brand in 2005, they turned to Parker Williams Design out of London. "Sainsbury's wanted a food brand that children ages 5 to 8 would eat and enjoy and that Mum could feel good about," says Tamara Williams, creative planner at Parker Williams.

Williams began by creating a brand mantra: "Clean plates, clean conscience." Then, the design team worked with a focus group and "mood boards" to determine what attributes each sample theme conveyed. The board that resonated the strongest with the focus group illustrated creativity—the kind kids might demonstrate in posting KEEP OUT signs on their bedroom doors. Clear, direct honesty also fared well—for example, "Eat a portion of [product] and give yourself five more minutes of energy to play football" garnered a positive response from the focus group.

The new packaging zeroed in on these key values when Sainsbury's launched its Sainsbury's Kids line in 2006. The palette for the background is yellow, signifying happiness and a positive image, and green, suggestive of health. Williams blurred the green slightly, throwing it out of focus to contrast with the clear image of the product and the child pictured on the package. The play of various contrasts worked well; the children pictured on the new packaging—often depicted holding a particular food right before their noses—move slightly out of focus, and their short hair didn't distract from the copy on the package.

Design Firm: Parker Williams
Location: London, England
Client: Sainsbury's Supermarkets
Industry: Retail

The lowercase kids is loosely based on Cocon Regular, in a reversed white with a slight ocher drop shadow. The *i*—which features a hand-drawn smiley face for the dot—and the ascender of the *k* were shortened to align better beneath Sainsbury's. The rest of the text is in Interstate, Sainsbury's corporate font.

The new packaging incorporates Sainsbury's standardized nutritional data and a heart-shaped green apple logo. The latter ties in to the supermarket's *be good to yourself* products, highlighting positive health messages.

Despite the consistent theme of the branding, the logos work on all kinds of products throughout the Sainsbury's Kids line, encouraging them to follow Sainsbury's slogan, "Try something new today." Parker Williams says that their packaging "appeals to kids because each one of them is different."

Design Firm: Cato Purnell Partners
Location: Collingwood, Australia
Client: ABC-TV
Industry: Television

Design Firm: William Fox Munroe
Location: Shillington, Penn.
Client: Hooked on Phonics
Industry: Education

Design Firm: William Fox Munroe
Location: Shillington, Penn.
Client: R.M. Palmer
Industry: Confectionery

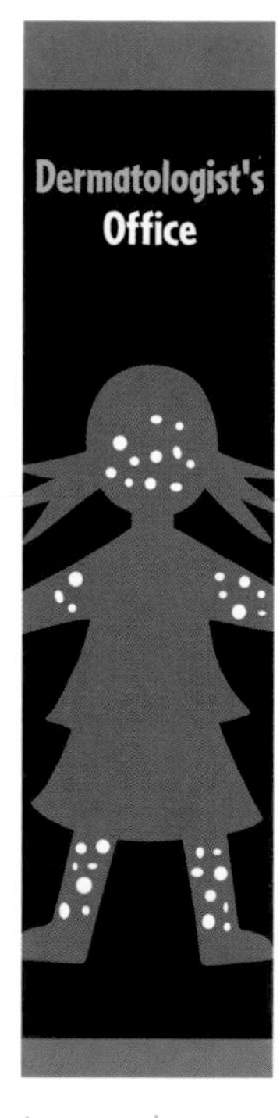

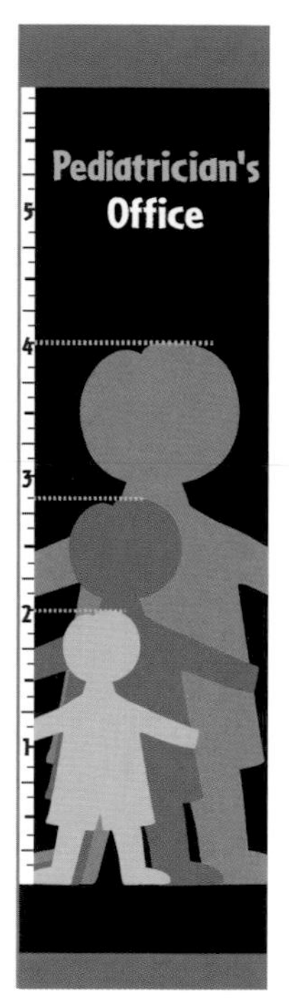

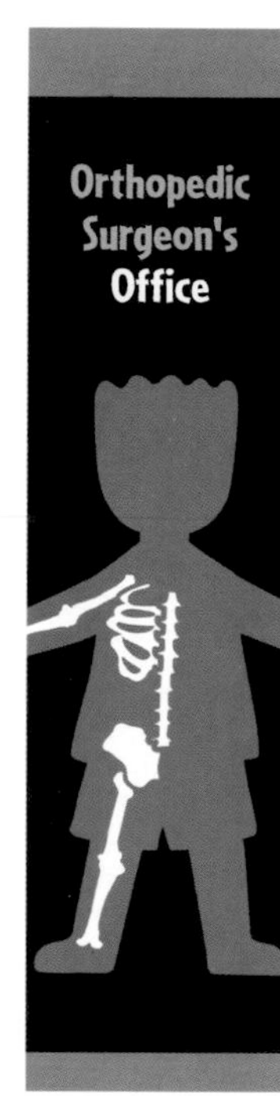

Design Firm: Pear Design
Location: Chicago, Ill.
Client: Architecture Is Fun
Industry: Children's Museum

mid-michigan
children's
museum

Design Firm: Pear Design
Location: Chicago, Ill.
Client: Mid Michigan Children's Museum
Industry: Children's Museum

Design Firm: Ripe Media
Location: Beverly Hills, Calif.
Client: The Wildwoods Foundation
Industry: Nonprofit

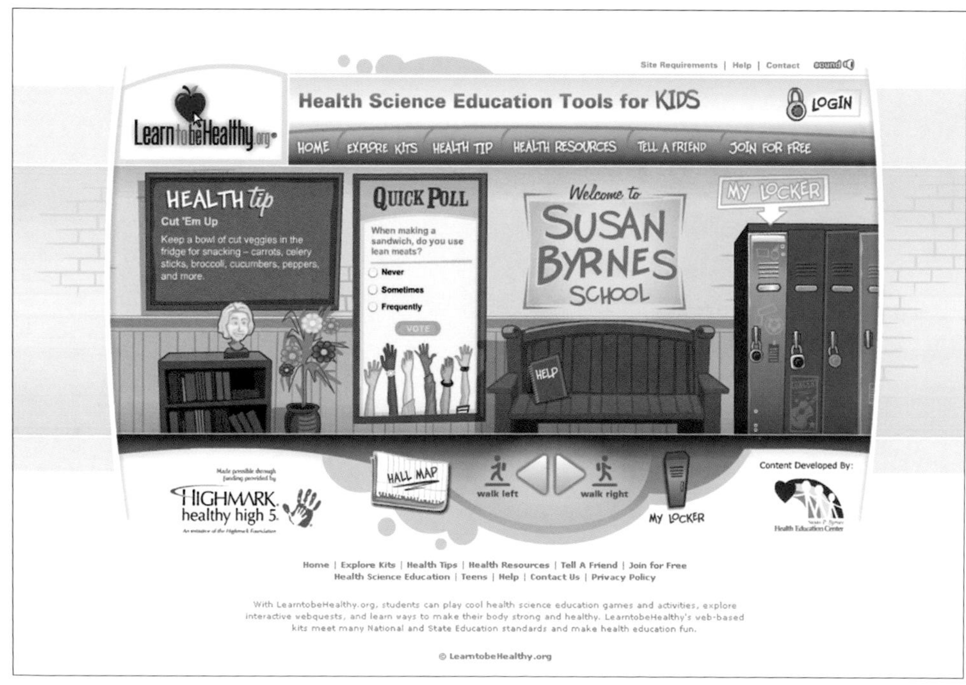

Design Firm: JPL Productions
Location: Harrisburg, Penn.
Client: Susan P. Byrnes Health Education Center
Industry: Health Education

Design Firm: Behavior Design
Location: New York, N.Y.
Client: 4kids Entertainment
Industry: Entertainment

Design Firm: Smith Design
Location: Glen Ridge, N.J.
Client: Hain-Celestial
Industry: Food & Beverage

Design Firm: Goodwin Design Group
Location: Media, Penn.
Client: Elmer's Products Inc.
Industry: Arts & Crafts

Dirty Laundry

Dirty Laundry, a children's apparel company based in Vancouver, British Columbia, is the brainchild of two self-described "dirty girls"—a designer and a businesswoman. Together, they created clothes that, while manufactured with very high quality materials and workmanship, feature completely unexpected designs—an appliquéd skull and crossbones next to pastels or camouflage, for example. Today, the brand is an international success story with a near-cult following, counting A-list parents Meg Ryan, Dustin Hoffman and Angelina Jolie as customers.

But in the beginning, when the company was ready to brand a rebellious look to match its irreverent name, the "dirty girls" turned to Byron Dowler, creative director of Coastlines Creative Group. As part of the branding package, Dowler delivered a logo, Web site, catalogue, stationery, a newsletter, hangtags and direct mail pieces—all designed with wit, intelligence and imagination to match the clothing with its desired attitude.

Dowler went for an industrial, old-school look for Dirty Laundry's wordmark, using the lowercase Typewriter font in simple, primary colors. For his centerpiece, he created an irreverent logo around one of the clothing's appliqués and then wove a story around it. The result was ACE, the sad-eyed wonder dog who's also "an international art thief that speaks French and jets around in his rocket ship." ACE is at the center, his head slightly rotated and surrounded by a tight, earthtone-colored circle. Dowler carried this attitude to the Web site. The kid talent has a deliberately tousled look, stylized via computer to make skin tones pale almost to the point of appearing gray, and clothing digitally superimposed.

The result is apparel for tweens and teens that is edgy yet urban with a cosmopolitan flair. Or, as Dowler put it, "bizarre and quirky, funky and sweet, but always cool."

Design Firm: Coastlines Creative Group
Location: Vancouver, B.C., Canada
Client: Dirty Laundry
Industry: Apparel

dirty laundry®

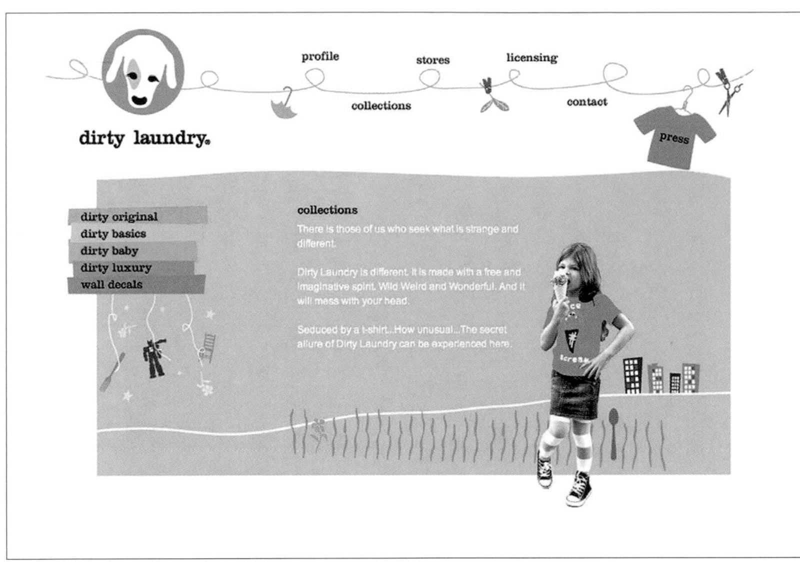

Design Firm: Kreaytive Studios
Location: Bangalore, India
Client: Kiddiecoo
Industry: Health & Beauty

Design Firm: Epos Inc.
Location: Hermosa Beach, Calif.
Client: Disney/ABC Cable Networks
Industry: Entertainment

Design Firm: Matcha Design
Location: Tulsa, Okla.
Client: Toys On Wings
Industry: Nonprofit

Design Firm: Riordon Design Group Inc.
Location: Oakville, Ont., Canada
Client: Vineyard Music
Industry: Christian Music

Design Firm: Cowan Design
Location: London, England
Client: Heinz
Industry: Grocery

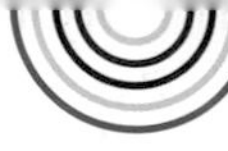

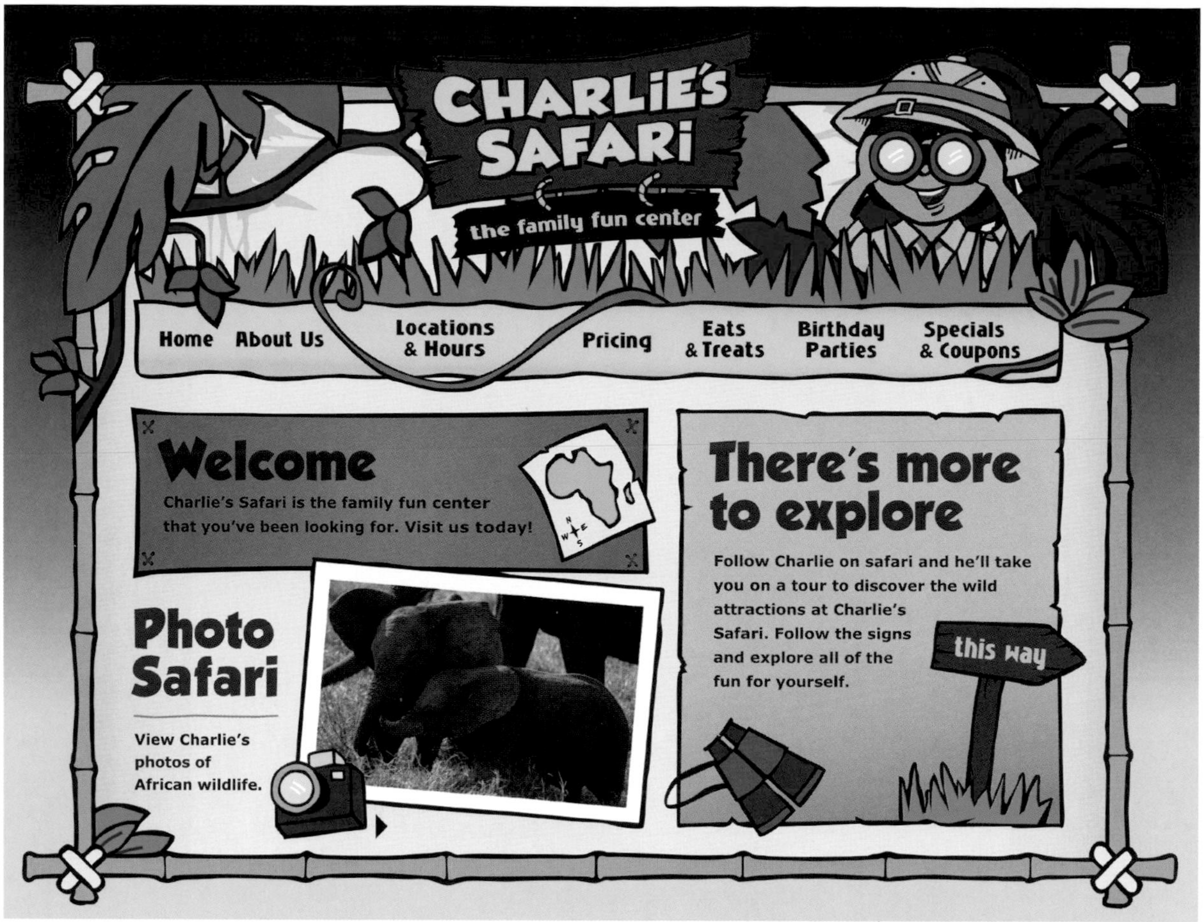
CHARLiE'S SAFARi
the family fun center
Home
About Us
Locations & Hours
Pricing
Eats & Treats
Birthday Parties
Specials & Coupons
Welcome
Charlie's Safari is the family fun center that you've been looking for. Visit us today!
There's more to explore
Follow Charlie on safari and he'll take you on a tour to discover the wild attractions at Charlie's Safari. Follow the signs and explore all of the fun for yourself.
this way
Photo Safari
View Charlie's photos of African wildlife.

Design Firm: Sungrafx
Location: Silverdale, Wash.
Client: Charlie's Safari
Industry: Retail

Suave
Kids
Smoothers
Suave
Kids
Smoothers
Suave
Kids
Smoothers
Suave
Kids
Smoothers

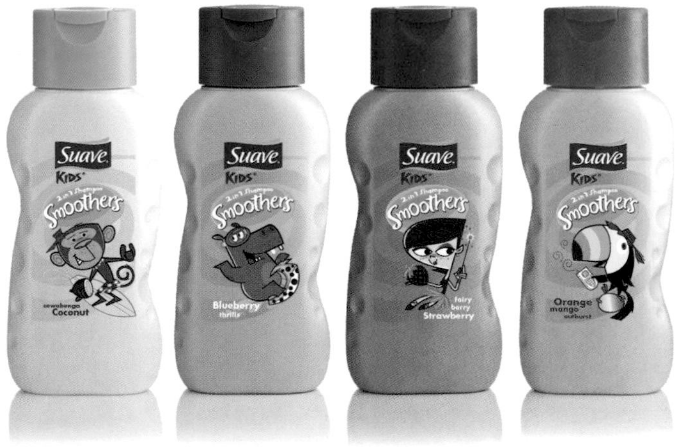

Design Firm: Optima Soulsight
Location: Highland Park, IL
Client: Unilever
Industry: Health and Beauty

Design Firm: YOE! Studio
Location: Peekskill, N.Y.
Client: Spin Master
Industry: Toys

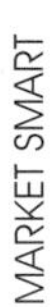

Design Firm: Jones Knowles Ritchie
Location: London, England
Client: Kraft
Industry: Food

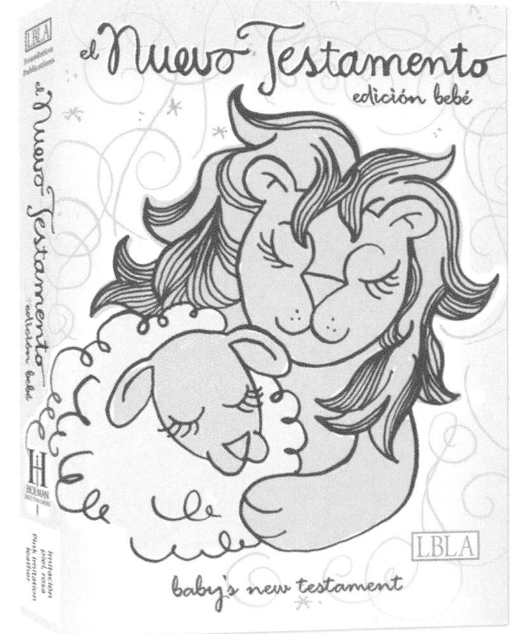

Design Firm: Anderson Design Group
Location: Nashville, TN
Client: Broadman & Holman Publishers
Industry: Product

CDN DENTAL ASSOCIATES

Design Firm: mad studios
Location: Hong Kong, China
Client: CDN Dental
Industry: Dentistry

TIPS FOR GOING TO THE DENTIST.
TIP#2:IMAGINE YOU ARE DOING
THE SAME THING TO HIM.
FOR MORE TIPS, ASK YOUR PARENTS TO MAKE AN APPOINTMENT.

CDN DENTAL ASSOCIATES

Good to Grow!

At a time when childhood obesity is growing at an alarming rate, the Association of Children's Museums (ACM) developed an initiative to help its member museums provide the public with information about healthy lifestyle choices.

Because the initiative needed to appeal to three particular audiences—children, their parents and children's museums across the U.S.—the ACM turned to Pittsburgh's Brady Communications for assistance with branding, naming and developing a comprehensive Web site for the program. Keeping in mind the three unique audiences, the Brady Communications team named the initiative *Good to Grow!*, suggesting that both the families and the museums could benefit—and grow—from involvement with the program. The team also designed a logo reflecting the energy and movement of healthy, growing kids.

It was crucial that the Web site be relevant and engaging for all. For children, the site needed to extend the local museum experience and teach healthy habits in a fun and exciting way; for parents, an additional resource for information on implementing healthy lifestyle choices in the home; and for ACM's member museums, a hub where program directors could exchange ideas and experiences about all aspects of family health programs and exhibits.

Focusing on the theme of good health, Brady Communications used the concepts of movement, activity and positive energy to inform the look and feel of the Web site. The color green was used to suggest growth—particularly as it relates to the goal of getting families to trade in their sedentary pursuits for active recreation in outdoor spaces such as parks and playgrounds. True to the initiative's focus, the ACM wanted to make sure families didn't stay on the *Good to Grow!* site too long—even if they were learning how to lead healthier lives.

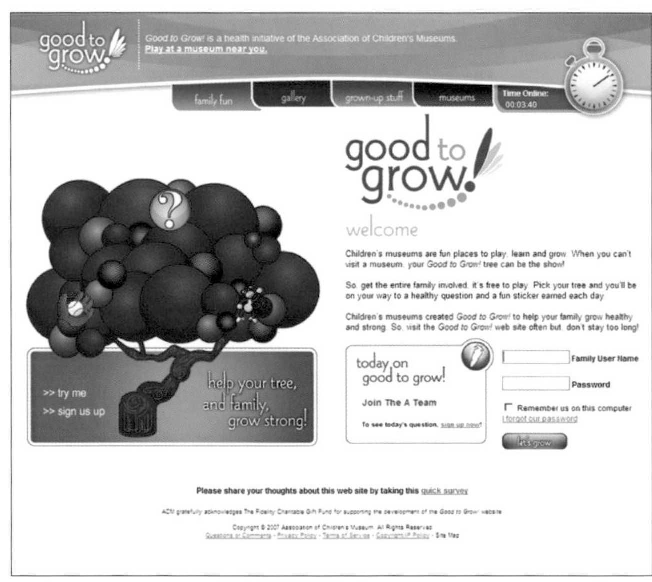

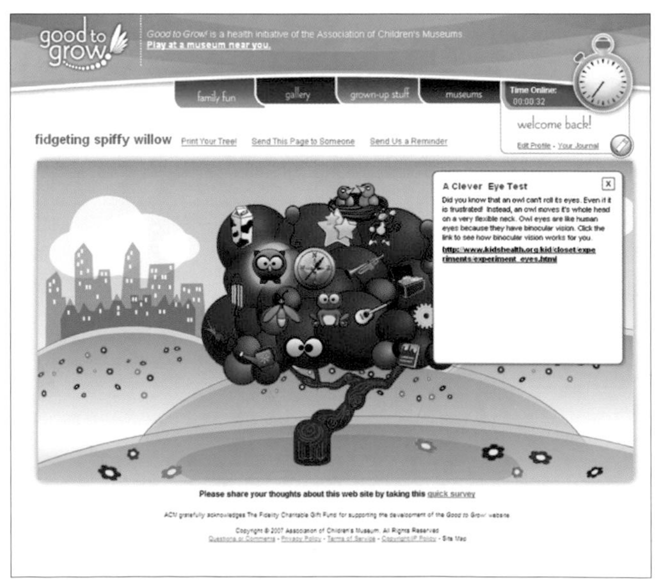

Design Firm: Brady Communications
Location: Pittsburgh, Penn.
Client: Good to Grow!
Industry: Museum

So Brady Communications developed a special interactive timer that tracked the amount of time users spent perusing the site, helping parents and kids monitor their time online.

Different sections of the Web site feature information targeted at each audience. The "Family Fun" section allows families to log in and create interactive *Good to Grow!* trees to represent their particular family's health. To decorate their tree, children and parents earn "stickers" for healthy lifestyle choices such as physical activity, balanced meals and reduced time in front of the TV or computer. "The Gallery" is where families can see an interesting array of *Good to Grow!* trees created by other families. In "Grown-Up Stuff," parents can find tips and tools to support their families' good health and connect with other parents online. In "Museums," families can learn about health-related events at their local children's museum, and the museums themselves can learn how other ACM member museums are implementing *Good to Grow!* activities, events and exhibits across the country.

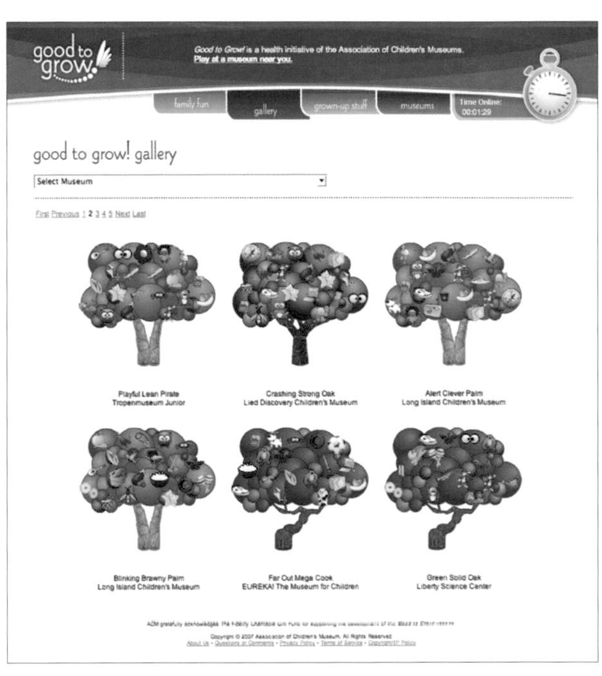

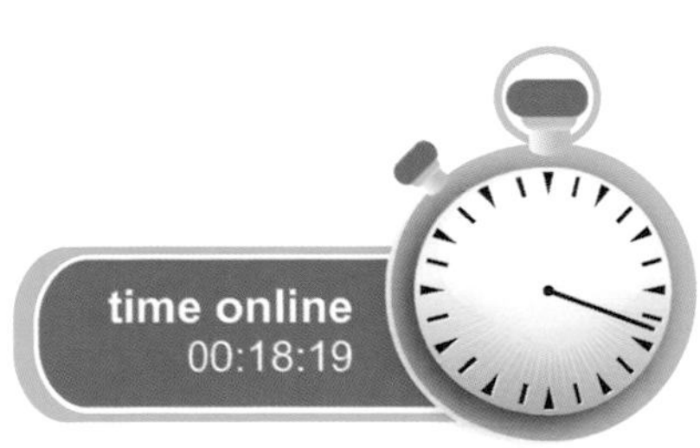

Tweens & Teens

Introduction by David Siegel

Let me introduce you to the most influential consumer in today's household: the tween. This person, age 8 to 12, is driven above all to confirm his or her identity and fit in. They're smart enough to know what they want and how to persuasively ask for it, but have little to no money with which to buy many things on their own yet. And, in today's world, the tween has become even more influential because today's Generation X mom—who does not want to waste her time or her money purchasing items that her tween won't eat, won't wear, won't like—actually involves her tween in her purchase decisions. It is not unusual for today's moms to ask her tween: "What should I get you from the store?" "What do you want for dinner?" "Where should we go to eat?" "Where should we go on vacation?" She'll even ask for their opinions on cars, detergents, even their next home!

And, when they shop together it really *is* a partnership. Using hidden cameras to watch moms and their tweens shop together in grocery stores, we often see Mom taking her tween to a store section and asking her child to choose which particular product he or she wants. Think that package design and in-store displays aren't critical here? Unfortunately, too many times tweens can't decide because they don't understand what the product looks like outside the box or how it might taste. For further proof of this, watch a mom take her tween to the Kool-Aid aisle and see how impatient she becomes because her tween can't figure out which package to buy or which flavor is what. Remember reading inequalities and instead show this tween market a neat character or an exciting graphic and watch them head for your package!

So, the tween is an important consumer segment, but who are these tweens and what do they look for? Well, the tween is in one heck of an identity crisis. He is too old to be a kid, but too young to be a teen. Too old to be considered a young child—or worse, a baby—yet too young to get into PG-13 movies. Too old to want to be totally dependent upon Mom and Dad's money, yet too young to get a job. His body has started to grow too fast, his voice is changing, and—hey, welcome to puberty! The fact is, tweens desperately want to know who they are and what they should be looking for. They want to make sure that they fit in...that they "belong" to the tween group. Design for this segment is critical because it is design that lets the tween know that the product is for them. Therein lies the golden rule for designing for tweens; tweens desperately search for items, packages and ads that help confirm who they are.

A few years ago, I was doing some work with a company considering launching flavored pancake syrups for tweens. When we discussed this concept with tweens, they were very excited

"They're smart enough to know what they want and how to persuasively ask for it, but have little to no money with which to buy many things on their own yet."

Dave is President and "Big Daddy" of WonderGroup, the largest independent U.S. agency specializing in marketing and advertising to today's moms and their kids.

Dave has spent the past 30 years immersed in youth and family marketing, advising some of the country's top corporations in such fields as: food & beverage, household cleaning products, health and beauty aids, toys, entertainment, clothing, retailing and others. He is a Gold Effie winner for his work on introducing and marketing the world's most successful leisure product of the '90s—the Super Soaker. He is an author of the *Great Tween Buying Machine* and *Marketing to the New Super Consumer: Mom & Kid.*

"While fun is extremely important to tweens, so are three other drivers: power, freedom and, especially, belonging."

over the idea—despite the fact that there already was a line of flavored pancake syrups available in the market. This was because the
packaging of the existing flavored syrups looked way too "adult" and the tweens felt that it wasn't for them. On the opposite end, any design using a cartoon character too "young" for our tween was marketing suicide. Mickey Mouse, Barney and most "roundish" characters scream "baby" to our tween.

While neither babies nor serious adults, tweens are fun-loving kids, looking for fun with the right attitude. YOE! Studio's snowboard designs are a wonderful example of showing the "right" kind of fun. So are Riordon Design's CD covers for Vineyard Music.

While fun is extremely important to tweens, so are three other drivers: power, freedom and, especially, belonging. Belonging is so important to this age group because they are in the process of leaving the safety of parents and family in favor of peer groups. Therefore, design elements that help tweens associate one or more of these drivers to your product are great helps. LPK's Jolly Rancher Rocks design (page 56) implies power and action in a wonderfully fun way for tweens. Hubbub.com by Justens Creative shows friendships, togetherness and belonging. Topps Town, the virtual world by Michael Eisner's Topps company, has it all with age-appropriate graphics, the promise of power in collecting and decorating, and belonging through a chat application. Naturally, actually incorporating tweens into the design is one of the best ways to reinforce that one's product is made for tweens. Kikibee Accessories (page 60) does this by showing the tween girls prominently on their web site. But remember one very big caveat in tween design: These consumers are still quite young, and they are still quite concrete in the way in which they process information. They do not have the mental ability to grasp abstract ideas or designs like adults can. In other words, visuals are everything! And keep the visuals somewhat simple. What they see is what they think. For a good example, take a look at the package design for Popsicle (page 51).

And now, a word about the teen consumer.

Teens are also very concerned with identity—less in confirming who they are but rather in shouting out what they want to be seen as. Peers are the most critical elements of their lives and they worry about what others are thinking about them. As part of this identity exhibitionism, this age segment looks for design that helps them be perceived as a guy or a girl much more than as "just a teen." Self-esteem, attractiveness and SEX dominate their thinking, and emotions and stress run at stratospheric heights.

Unlike the tween segment, this group is into abstract, conceptual thinking. It is not as important to make it so obvious what your product offering is; don't scream it—rather, use design to draw them in. Take a look at the layout and design of Spencer's Gifts (page 52) and Hot Topic by JGA (page 44); you can just feel the energy and attitude in the environment!

80 percent of all global brands now utilize a special "tween strategy" to market to the preteen market.[6]

In 2005, kids age 8-18 managed to get 8.5 hours of media exposure in 6.5 hours per day, every day—more than any of them spent in the classroom.[7]

The size of the U.S. tween market is 20.9 million— about two-thirds the entire population of Canada.[8]

52 percent of kids age 12-21 consider friends' recommendations when making a purchase.[9]

The average weekly allowance for children age 6-14 is $7; the average weekly allowance for teens age 15-17 is $21.[10]

Basic Facts About: Tweens & Teens

Rules to follow when Marketing to Tweens & Teens:

1. **Make it look like it's just for them.**
   Tweens are in a transition away from being the baby and toward being the grownup, so include cues, designs, fonts and illustrations that let tweens know your product is for kids like them—not just adults, not babies. Tweens look for reassurance in the package design elements and overall communications to tell them that the product is made for kids their age.

2. **Communicate through visuals.**
   Tweens are extraordinarily dependent on visuals, especially since their reading skills may not be up to par across the board. If your product features different flavors and different shapes, show them that! Remember, tweens are primarily concrete in their information processing capabilities, so seeing is understanding to them.

3. **Keep it looking new.**
   Good news—tweens like to try new things. Bad news—tweens like to try new things. If you don't stay new, you are no longer interesting to tweens. Package designs and communication efforts should clearly feature new varieties, limited edition SKUs or new promotional offerings on a timely basis. If not, tweens will look elsewhere for something else they'll perceive as new.

4. **Make it fun.**
   While tweens are driven by four basic motivators (power, freedom, fun and belonging), the trump card is definitely fun. Colors, fonts and illustrations must reassure tweens that they'll have fun with your product. If not, there are plenty of other tween-oriented products that they can choose over yours.

5. **Mom matters.**
   Much of tween purchasing relies on a joint decision with—or, many times, obtaining permission from—Mom. If possible, include some information important to moms. Prominently featuring vitamin content, nutritional benefits, even mom-targeted promotions will go a long way helping with parental buy-in. And, contrary to what you might have heard, putting such information on packaging will not turn off the tween.

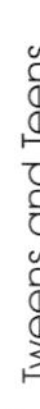

Design Firm: Brady Communications
Location: Pittsburgh, Penn.
Client: Tippmann Sports
Industry: Paintball

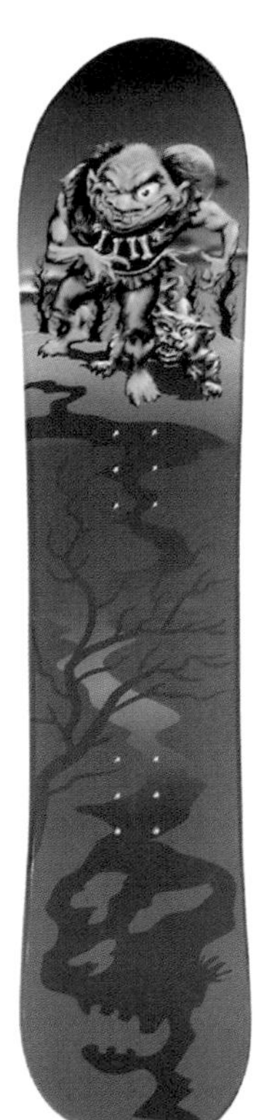

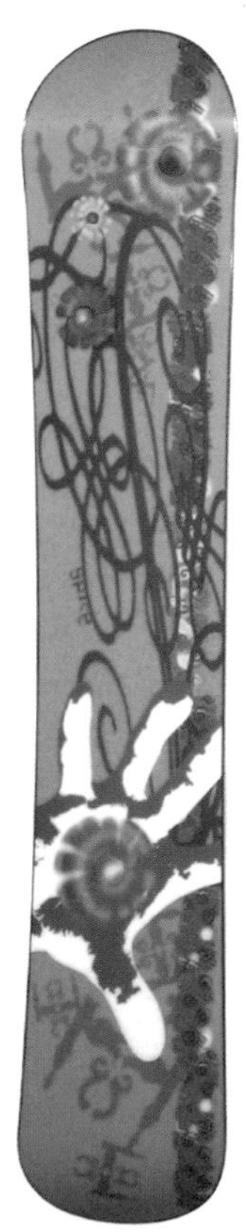

Design Firm: YOE! Studio
Location: Peekskill, N.Y.
Client: Snowjam
Industry: Sporting Goods

Design Firm: JGA
Location: Southfield, Mich.
Client: Hot Topic
Industry: Retail

HT
E204
HOT TOPIC®
everything about the music
NEW RELEASES
$9.99
NEW FOUND GLORY 9.19
MUSHROOMHEAD 9.19
SAOSIN 9.26
HT
E204

Singing the Body Eclectic

Nowhere is the anxiety associated with being on the far end of society's body-image spectrum more pronounced than in adolescence. That's why Merrill Guerra, founder of RealKidz Clothing in Ypsilanti, Mich., turned to Scott Pryor of Ann Arbor's Pryor Design to help form a brand identity for her line of clothing for girls who don't fit the petite pop star wardrobe—literally. "Merrill really hit it," Pryor says of Guerra's solution born of her quest for age-appropriate fashion for her own daughter.

Using Guerra's original tagline, "Life styles for every body," Pryor set out to do "anything we could to make this an inspiring, youthful and uplifting brand... custom tailored just for them." In this case, "them" refers to young ladies whose fashion options are too often limited because of their body size and shape. To this end, Pryor developed messaging—seen throughout the RealKidz Web site and on its in-store signage—designed to empower its young clientele, juxtaposed with color and black-and-white photography of real girls completely at ease in their RealKidz attire. "'Finally... a line of clothing that's as real as me.' Our goal was to really be immediate with the tone of voice and how the photography is presented."

Unifying these positive messages and photographic images is one element that runs consistently throughout all RealKidz media: an artifact that Pryor describes as "between an asterisk and a flower. It's a neat little energy burst with a life of its own." This energy extends to both kids and their parents, including Pryor himself. "For kids, it's so fresh and youthful, and the same things work with moms. If it's really great for my kids, I see it as well."

Design Firm: Pryor Design
Location: Ann Arbor, Mich.
Client: RealKidz
Industry: Apparel

Besides the Web site, Pryor also designed stationery, business cards, in-store signage ("brand panels" that could also double as magazine ads) and hangtags emblazoned with affirming mantras. Even the bright color scheme—vibrant magenta, yellow, chartreuse and cyan—seems infused with positive feeling. But by using the Bryant typeface, Pryor indeed kept things real—and simple. "A natural typeface [for such a campaign] would be a curlicue, but we wanted to let the other elements come through," he says. "Fun, rounded and approachable; clean and simple. They all fit together in the scheme—font, colors, rounded building blocks across the board."

Pryor's "building blocks" approach imposes order on a growing brand. "We've developed enough colors that we could define something new for a [proposed] boys' line," he says. "We can modify the logo to be more gender-specific. The building blocks are built... to be kind of a mosaic, in a simple but graphic way. We felt we could evolve it."

This evolution, however far-reaching, never strays too far from its roots: the need for growing girls to be listened to, understood and affirmed. The slogans "work on multiple levels," Pryor says. *"I am real.* It's a thought bubble. Like the clothes talking—as well as the person."

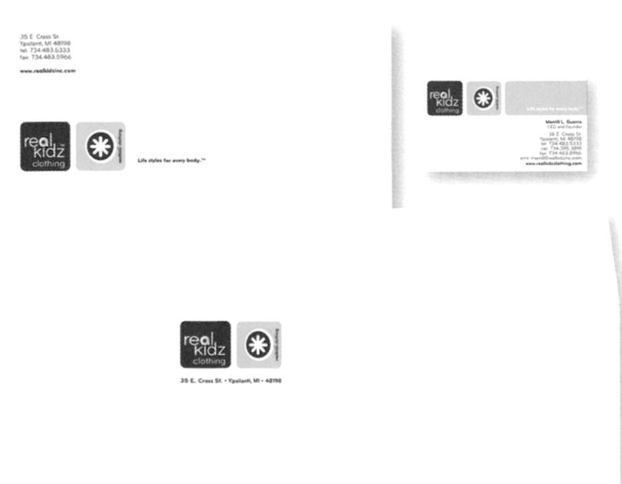

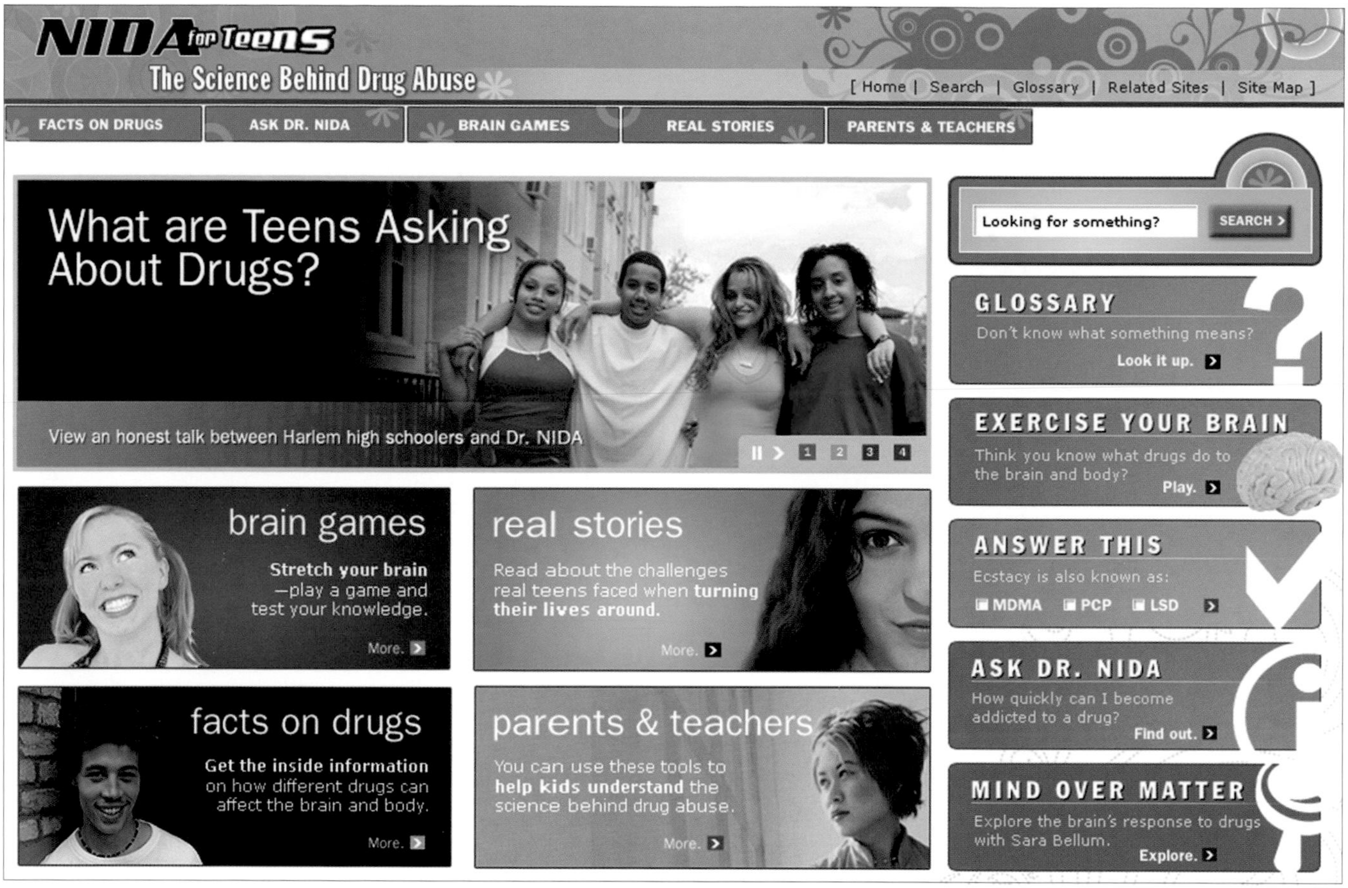

NIDA for Teens
The Science Behind Drug Abuse
[Home | Search | Glossary | Related Sites | Site Map]

FACTS ON DRUGS | ASK DR. NIDA | BRAIN GAMES | REAL STORIES | PARENTS & TEACHERS

What are Teens Asking About Drugs?

View an honest talk between Harlem high schoolers and Dr. NIDA

1 2 3 4

Looking for something? SEARCH

GLOSSARY
Don't know what something means?
Look it up.

brain games
Stretch your brain —play a game and test your knowledge.
More.

real stories
Read about the challenges real teens faced when turning their lives around.
More.

EXERCISE YOUR BRAIN
Think you know what drugs do to the brain and body?
Play.

ANSWER THIS
Ecstacy is also known as:
MDMA PCP LSD

facts on drugs
Get the inside information on how different drugs can affect the brain and body.
More.

parents & teachers
You can use these tools to help kids understand the science behind drug abuse.
More.

ASK DR. NIDA
How quickly can I become addicted to a drug?
Find out.

MIND OVER MATTER
Explore the brain's response to drugs with Sara Bellum.
Explore.

Design Firm: Jacob Tyler Creative Group
Location: San Diego, Calif.
Client: NIDA
Industry: Public Service

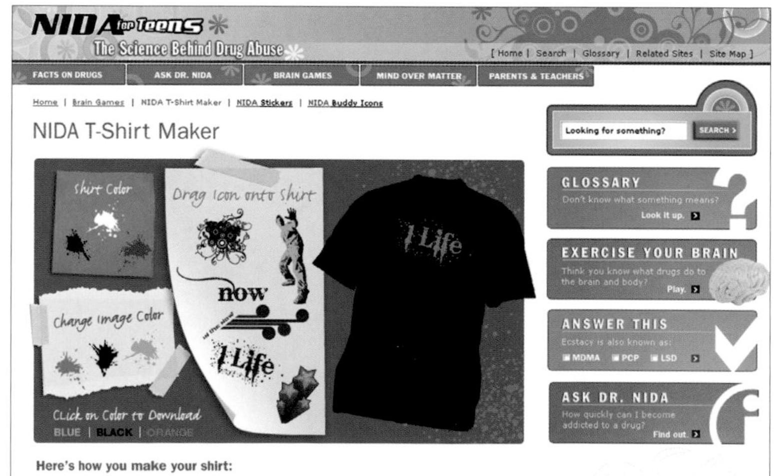

Design Firm: WonderGroup
Location: Cincinnati, Ohio
Client: The Topps Company Inc.
Industry: Sports Trading Cards

Design Firm: Jones Knowles Ritchie
Location: London, England
Client: Britvic
Industry: Food & Beverage

Design Firm: Rhiannon Cunag
Location: Scottsdale, AZ.
Client: Scholastic
Industry: Publishing

Design Firm: BBR Creative
Location: Lafayette, LA.
Client: LPSO
Industry: Public Service

Design Firm: Smith Design
Location: Glen Ridge, N.J.
Client: SAKAR
Industry: Electronics

Design Firm: William Fox Munroe
Location: Shillington, Penn.
Client: R.M. Palmer
Industry: Confectionery

Design Firm: Smith Design
Location: Glen Ridge, N.J.
Client: Unilever/Popsicle
Industry: Food

SPENCER'S
enter
1947

Design Firm: JGA
Location: Southfield, Mich.
Client: Spencer's
Industry: Retail

The Whole 110 Yards

Lacrosse can be a fierce sport—"attackman" is one position—and while there may be nothing "girly" about it, female teens who want to make a statement turn to STX, maker of lacrosse sticks for both the men's and women's market. Design director Greg Bennett and production director David Griffiths, of Baltimore-based agency Siquis, came to appreciate the game and its equipment the more they worked to develop sticks and graphics for their young, athletic market.

"The unifying theme was to enhance performance features which differed from stick to stick," says Bennett. "This line of lacrosse stick graphics was designed to appeal to teenage girls who want their sporting equipment to make as bold a statement as everything else in their lives." The sticks aren't your typical plain netted shafts, either. With a rich metallic palette, unlikely color combinations and truly intricate designs including chevrons, abstract florals and sharp directionals, Bennett and Griffiths developed a variety of aesthetically appealing shafts that would look equally at home on equipment associated with fast-moving activities such as surfing, skateboarding, kayaking and skiing. To illustrate each stick's unique "performance features," Siquis used a wide variety of colors and graphics to highlight attributes, singularly or in combination with one another, important to people who know the sport best: its players. Bennett lists "molded grips, dual molded grips, twisted grips [and] a specialized shape grip for enhanced handling" as unique features of STX's line.

Design Firm: Siquis
Location: Baltimore, Md.
Client: STX Lacrosse
Industry: Sports Equipment

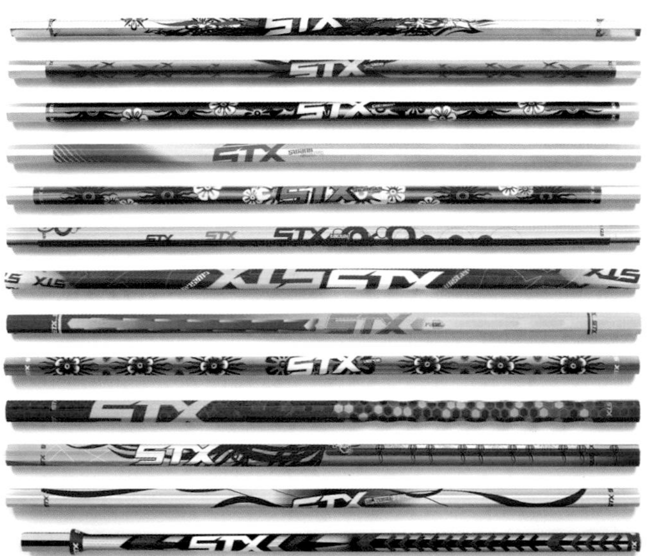

Designing a more dynamic stick wasn't all Siquis signed on to do for the gear company. "For STX Lacrosse we designed a full line of men's and women's stick graphics, posters and advertising," Bennett says. "For STX Field Hockey, we designed full lines of women's stick graphics for both their wood and composite lines, trade catalogs, advertising and a Web site." The images used in the marketing materials suggest more than just a simple piece of sports equipment. In one image, parallel sticks suggest a formidable offense, while in another the field hockey sticks curl to a gently rounded end. Still, Bennett says, there is tradition behind the color prism as Siquis designed for sticks in materials old and new: "We had to re-examine the wood stick line to make it more appealing even though composite sticks are more advanced," he says of STX's wood field hockey line. Siquis achieved this through "a fun use of icons and color" to convey each stick's personality and uniqueness.

But it's not all sticks and heads; one of the many catalogs Bennett designed for STX Field Hockey features the tagline, "You want some of this?" and a female player, field hockey stick slung over one shoulder and her opposite hand defiantly on her hip. And if it that player looks like an Amazon warrior, all the better. According to Bennett, the aggressive image is "designed to capture the... attitude behind the STX field hockey player." Another field hockey catalog featured Tara Jelley—a player Bennett compares to Michael Jordan in the field hockey arena—Siquis used her image in STX brochures to accentuate the attitude lacrosse players and fans best embody. "We hired Brion McCarthy of Apparitionstudio.com to ensure our photography portrayed Tara's true characteristics." he says. "Extreme close-ups, untraditional perspective, intense and confident" describe both the shots and the spirit of the STX customer—one both the client and agency understand intimately and summed up in the tagline, "At STX, we're players just like you."

Design Firm: Jostens Creative
Location: Minneapolis, Minn.
Client: Jostens
Industry: Manufacturing

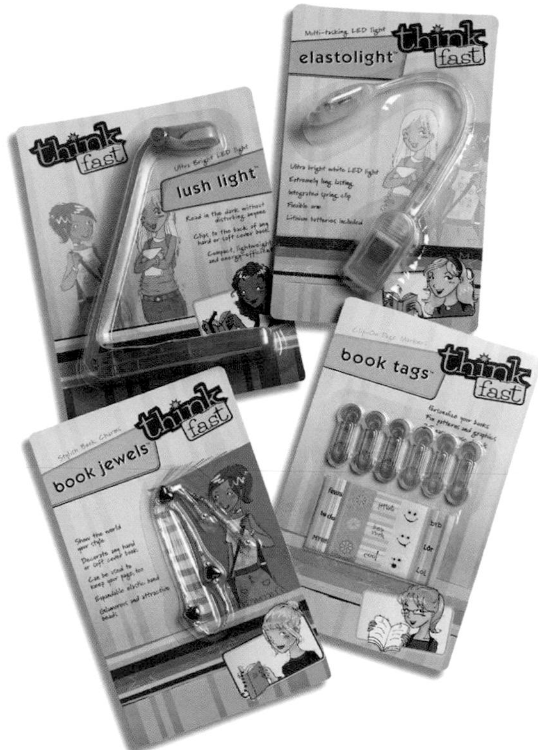

Design Firm: Silver Creative Group
Location: Norwalk, Conn.
Client: Zelco
Industry: Electronics

Design Firm: LPK
Location: Cincinnati, Ohio
Client: Hershey
Industry: CPG

Design Firm: Reactivity Studio
Location: Austin, Texas
Client: Wear Me Out Boys Clothing
Industry: Retail

Design Firm: Dunn and Rice Design, Inc.
Location: Rochester, NY
Client: Hasbro
Industry: Toys

Design Firm: JGA
Location: Southfield, Mich.
Client: Kira Plastinina
Industry: Retail Apparel

Design Firm: Lewis Moberly
Location: London, England
Client: The Girl Company
Industry: Retail

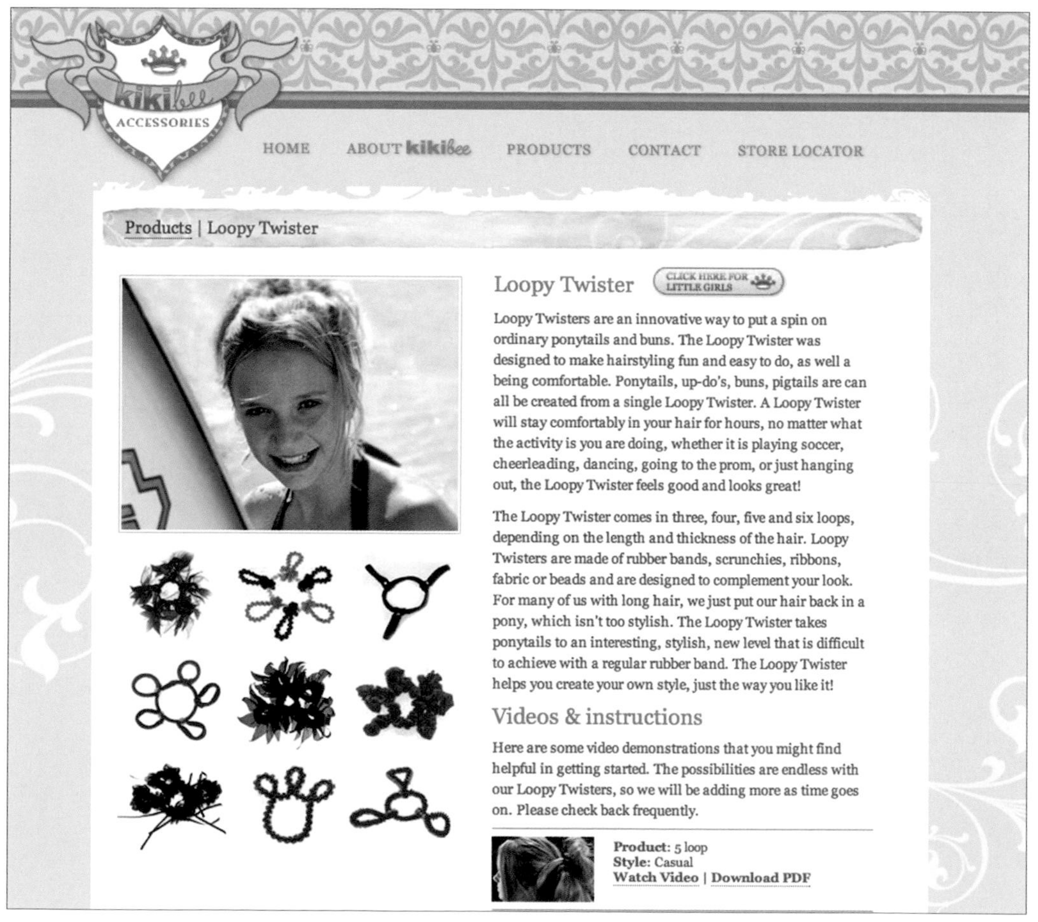

Design Firm: Session Creative
Location: Cotati, Calif.
Client: Kikibee Accessories
Industry: Fashion Accessories

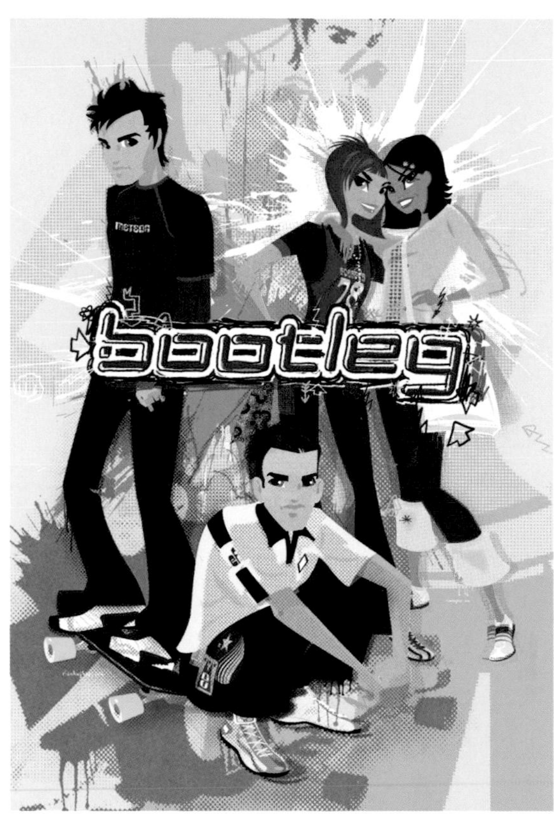

Design Firm: Device
Location: London, England
Client: Clark's Shoes
Industry: Retail

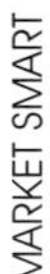

Design Firm: element3media
Location: Phoenix, Ariz.
Client: University of Advancing Technology
Industry: Education

Design Firm: element3media
Location: Phoenix, Ariz.
Client: University of Advancing Technology
Industry: Education

Lightning in a Jar

For many adults, a firefly evokes memories of freedom and discovery—attributes that were, to Jeff Zwerner of Factor Design out of San Francisco, a perfect match for a cell phone for kids in the 8-to-12 age bracket. "The original identity established by the founder had very 'Star Trek'-type typography, purple and green, very male, very aggressive," he says of the concept that Firefly Mobile came to him with. "I said, 'Why don't you use a firefly?'" But when the client balked, citing the, well, *bugness* of its mascot, Zwerner persisted. "That's the magic of a firefly. It doesn't have to be rendered correctly, but how your imagination takes you."

Firefly Mobile pioneered the cell phone made especially for tweens and how they live now, so there was no precedent about trying to sell such an object. "There was a lively debate about marketing phones to teens and younger [kids]," he says. "It's an easy play to talk about the fear factor with parents, but we never went into why you need to be in touch. Our biggest challenge was how we could appeal to both kids and adults. This was smarter, and we gave people more credit as to why they needed this."

To appeal to both generations, Firefly Mobile asked Zwerner to create a specific personality for the brand—and they thought big. "We created an entire brand language," he says, "everything from the identity itself to the Web site, packaging and postcards. When [Firefly] launched the product, their objective was to partner with Target and with a major carrier, preferably Cingular." The original photography, which Factor directed, features tweens leaping through the air among colorful bubbles—an image perfectly at home in a Target ad. It paid off. Six months after Firefly approached Factor, the phones were on the shelf at 1,400 Target stores, with Cingular as the carrier of choice for the fledgling brand.

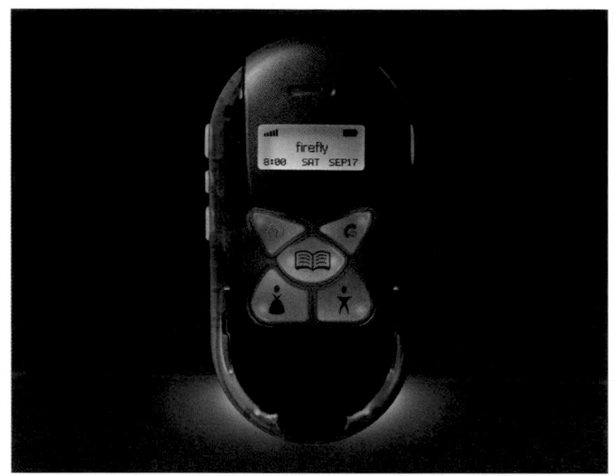

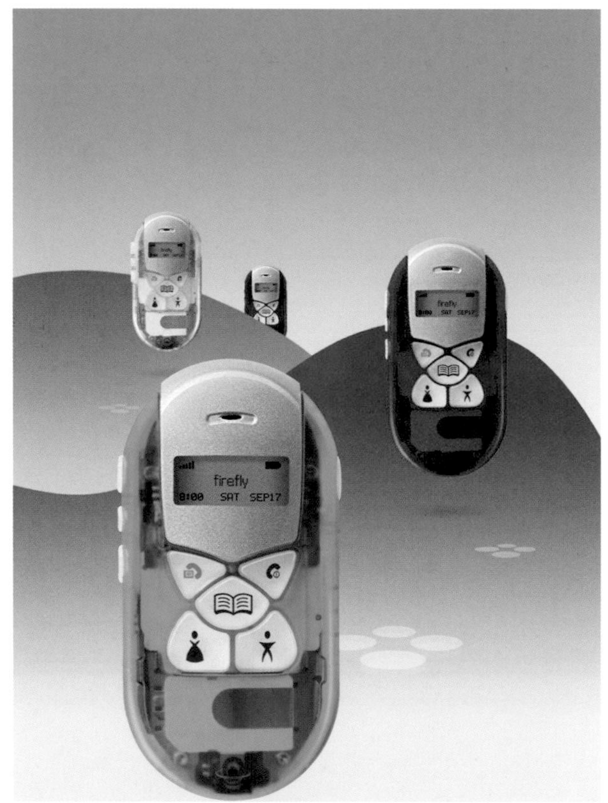

Design Firm: Factor Design
Location: San Francisco, Calif.
Client: Firefly Mobile
Industry: Mobile Communications

But would it sell? Firefly's heart went out to potential partners before their phones even went to market. "We did an internal guidebook about how the company would grow," Zwerner says. "It talked about their core vision and values: 'Our philosophy is…' It was a very purposeful product interaction that showed how it can scale to other markets and offerings." With Target and Cingular in place, the next step was to win over the target market—and their wallet-wielding parents. "We had every intention of taking it to the consumer," Zwerner says, "but the challenge of the program was this bifocal marketing to parents and kids—to create an object of desire for the kids, and to get to the parents, who are the gatekeepers. We wanted to make them comfortable with that way of life, the technology, how it works."

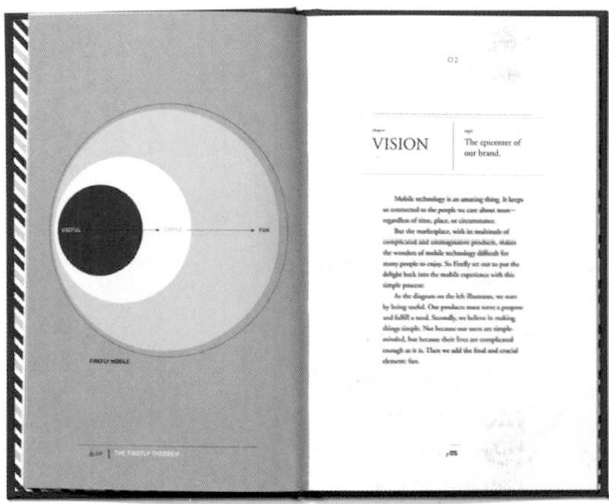

How it works is unlike most tween "objects of desire"; for one thing, it has "a lot of security. No keypad—you can make calls only to numbers already in the phone's directory, which is a laborious process to get into," says Zwerner. "You can get calls from people already in the phone book—that's an option you can turn on and off—but there's no texting, no pictures [function]." This didn't stop the kids in the focus groups from convincing Mom and Dad to give the Firefly phone a chance. "We didn't need to pander to the kids, but we gave them the tools to say, 'I want this,' 'I need this,' 'You should feel comfortable that I'm talking only to certain people,'" Zwerner says. "In the focus groups, kids still wanted a full-feature cell phone, but when there were no adults in the room, it's pretty remarkable how they rationalized [this phone] and then parroted it back to adults in language Mom and Dad would understand. And the parents don't want to say no to their kids."

As coin-operated pay phones disappear from the landscape and even toddlers play with computers, Firefly's Factor-created slogan, "The Mobile Phone for Mobile Kids," respects the tweens' intelligence and, yes, freedom. "They're so adept these days," Zwerner says. "The equivalent to having a quarter is having a cell phone in their bag."

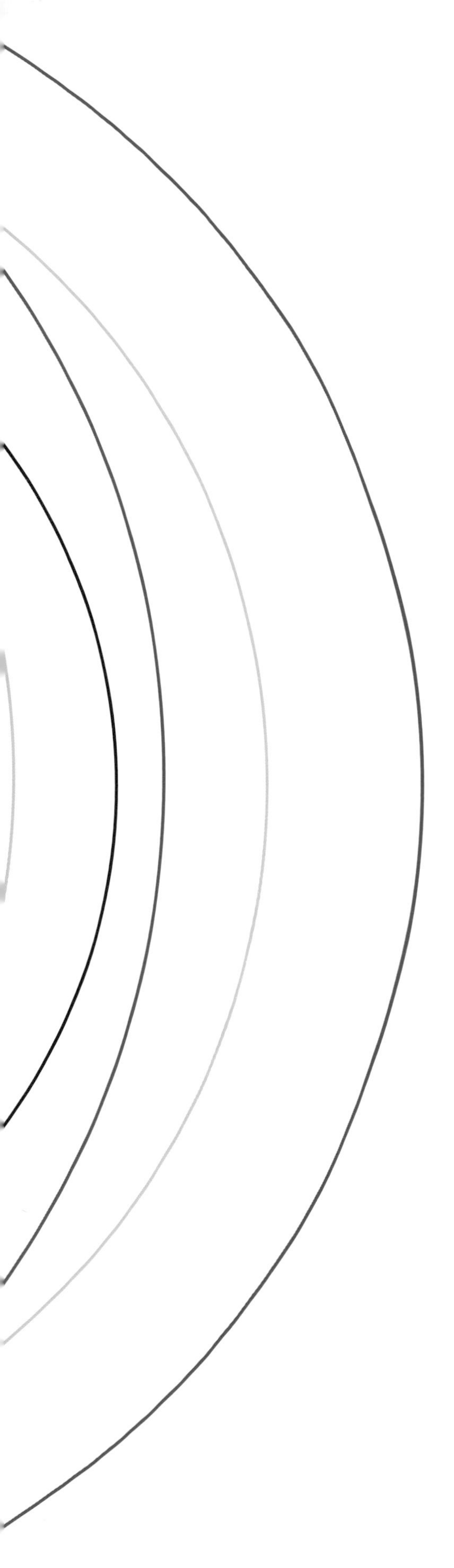

3

Generations X and Y

Introduction by David Bonner

Meet Generation X: officially nameless. If you're a marketer, don't expect a handshake.

Economically, X is the bear market. In fact, we're sometimes called "baby busters," as in the bust after the baby boom—that postwar demographic tsunami that brought forth Elvis and free love, but left us with disco and HIV/AIDS. Despite our parents' use of "The Pill," Xers arrived to break up the party around 1965. The only real identity X enjoys is the feeling that we'll be overwhelmed by the wave of social problems left for us to solve. We were the first latchkey generation, with only "Happy Days" to offer the rare glimpse into our parents' and grandparents' values. We were raised on MTV, movies about devil children, "Saturday Night Live," *Star Wars* and Nixon.

"The way to market to Gen X is by 'anti-marketing.' Simply put, take everything you've known about selling something and turn it on its head."

The way to market to Gen X is by "anti-marketing." Simply put, take everything you've known about selling something and turn it on its head. Angry and impotent, X expresses itself in slasher movies and satires. If a boomer feels horrified or nostalgic about a topic, Gen X will turn it into a joke.

David Bonner is an insatiably curious ad man. Highlights of his thrilling 14-year career include new business development, chief creative officer duties, all the copywriting ranks, account planner and account executive. Agency stops have included the multinational powerhouses JWT Chicago and BBDO Toronto, as well as independent boutiques GJP and Doe-Anderson. His work has been recognized at Cannes, The One Show, The ADDYs and the Clios. David is currently SVP, Executive Creative Director at St. John + Partners in Jacksonville, Florida.

Less is more for Gen X. Hide your capitalist intentions behind music videos, comedic sketches, satirical genres and outrageous hyperboles. And be quick about it. We devour information in sound bite-sized chunks.

Xers know from our alphabetical order that if this isn't the end, we're close. The Internet is our only accomplishment, although it will take Gen Y to put it to real use.

Gen Y, or the millennials, are the children of the boomers. Psychologically, they're much simpler. Y inherited the boomers' optimistic sense of entitlement and privilege, juiced with the global access and power of the Internet. They have no memory of the Cold War or Vietnam; 9/11 and the War on Terror have been the defining events of their very busy lives. This peer group is cemented together with emotional Super Glue and technology. Like a massive rubber band, they are stretched wide with massive potential energy and power that may yet save the world from itself.

"Social marketing and self-fulfillment is the key to Gen Y. They expect a true dialogue with a brand, and they'll be happy to start the conversation on their own terms."

Having had ready access to cutting-edge technology from birth, iTunes, Napster and YouTube taught Y that instant gratification was just a download away. If X uses e-mail, Y uses IM. X had yearbooks, but Y has Facebook and MySpace. X still rode bikes to school, but Y moves in minivan swarms that can deliver marketing phenomena like *Harry Potter* and MP3 players. Whatever political direction they choose, Gen Y could move our system from a distant representational democracy to something far more involved and self-directed.

Because of Y's peer group cohesion, they crave a strong opposing need for personal identity. Y believes they are entitled to self-actualization and understands brand personalities better than anyone. After all, they've crafted their very own personal brand identities online. They are potent creators in all forms.

Social marketing and self-fulfillment is the key to Gen Y. They expect a true dialogue with a brand, and they'll be happy to start the conversation on their own terms. If you're worthy, they might even invite you to be their friend, so market to Y honestly, authentically and individually. Right or wrong, they'll be sure to tell their friends.

Generation X, with approximately 30 percent with a bachelor's degree or higher in 2003, is the most educated generation ever.[11]

While the 30-to-44 segment traditionally has spent the most on food, housing, personal care products, entertainment and cars, they will be overtaken in 2009 by their parents' generation in overall spending power as the Generation X age bracket declines by 6 percent.[12]

Annually, Generation X members spend 18 percent more on luxury goods—and 10 percent more on everything else—than do baby boomers.[13]

Generation X spends approximately 12 percent more than other typical American consumers on entertainment—and about 9 percent more on food.[14]

Out of nearly 50 million members, 62 percent of Generation X is married, and 29.7 million are parents.[15]

Basic Facts About: Generations X and Y

Rules to follow when Marketing to Generation X:

1. **They are scattered and skeptical, so get to the point.** They don't read, they scan.

2. **X and Y are the real owners of the Internet,** making them addicts of information, networking and immediate gratification.

3. **With X and Y, what you see is what you get.** Keep it real and personal.

4. **They are genuinely pissed off over the boomers' journey down the yellow brick road.** So yes, Toto, there's a reason to use marketing lingo that's "edgy." It's to subconsciously slice open Dorothy's gluttonous throat.

5. **Programmed problem-solvers since Pong,** visual riddles are their lingua franca.

Rules to follow when Marketing to Generation Y:

1. **Born between 1977 and 1994, Generation Y makes up over** 20% of the U.S population, and includes over 70 million people.

2. **Generation Y is more than three times the size of** Generation X.

3. **40% of U.S teens have part-time jobs**, with an average of $100 in disposable income a week.

4. **This generation is more apt to trust** parents (86 percent), teachers (86 percent) and the police (83 percent) than music celebrities (35 percent) and athletes (30 percent). *

5. **Gen Y is ambitious, hopeful and in a hurry.** They are action-oriented, direct and excellent multi-taskers, a result of growing up in the age of technology. 75-90% have a computer at home.

*Applied Research & Consulting LLC.

Design Firm: Piotrowski DSN
Location: Warsaw, Poland
Client: Lay's
Industry: Food & Beverage

Design Firm: Lotus Child
Location: San Francisco, Calif.
Client: SmartsCo
Industry: Game

Design Firm: Geyrhalter Design
Location: Santa Monica, Calif.
Client: John Varvatos
Industry: Fashion

Design Firm: Philippe Becker
Location: San Francisco, Calif.
Client: Cost Plus World Market
Industry: Health & Beauty

Design Firm: BIRD
Location: Hollywood, Calif.
Client: Speed
Industry: Entertainment/Broadcast Cable

Design Firm: BIRD
Location: Hollywood, Calif.
Client: G4
Industry: Entertainment/Broadcast Cable

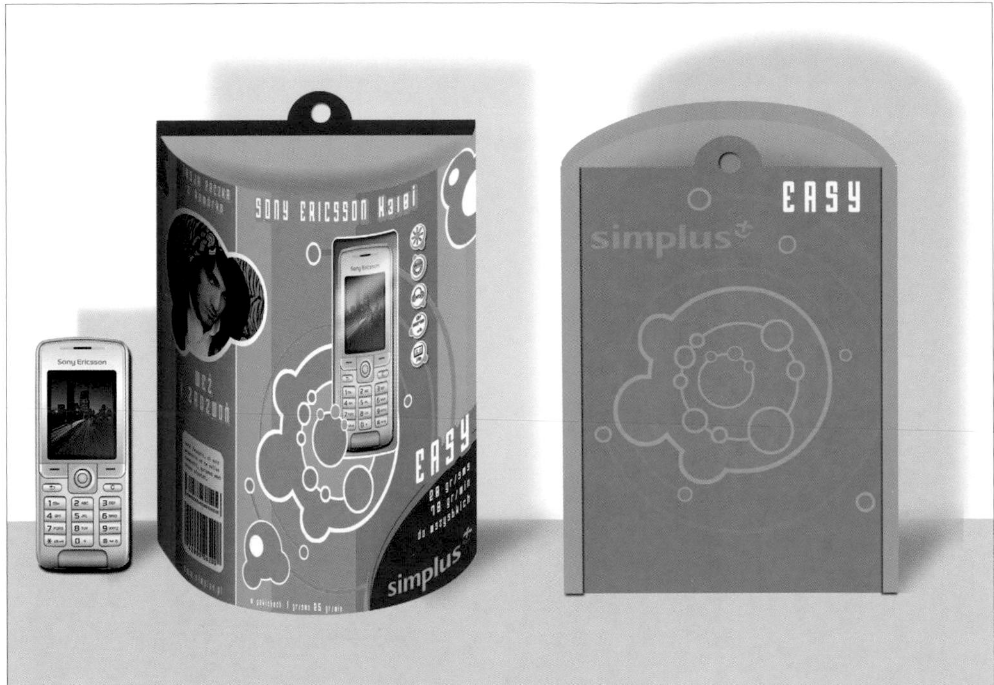

Design Firm: Piotrowski DSN
Location: Warsaw, Poland
Client: Simplus
Industry: Telecommunications

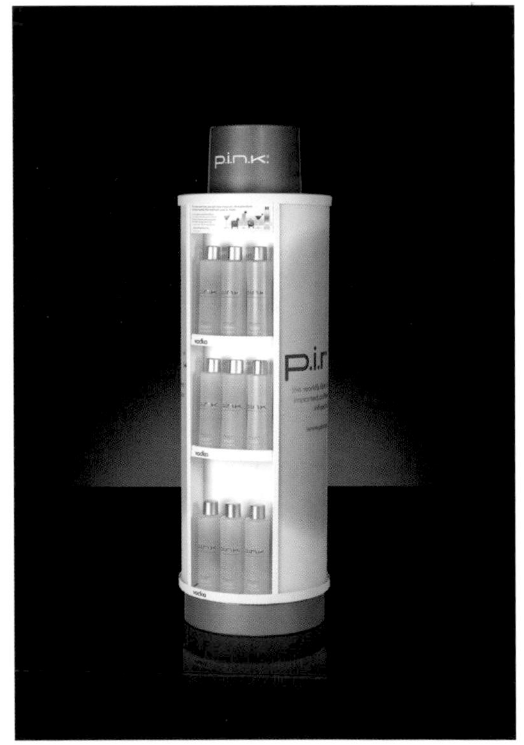

Design Firm: Bailey Brand Consulting
Location: Plymouth Meeting, Penn.
Client: The p.i.n.k. Spirits Company
Industry: Distilled Spirits

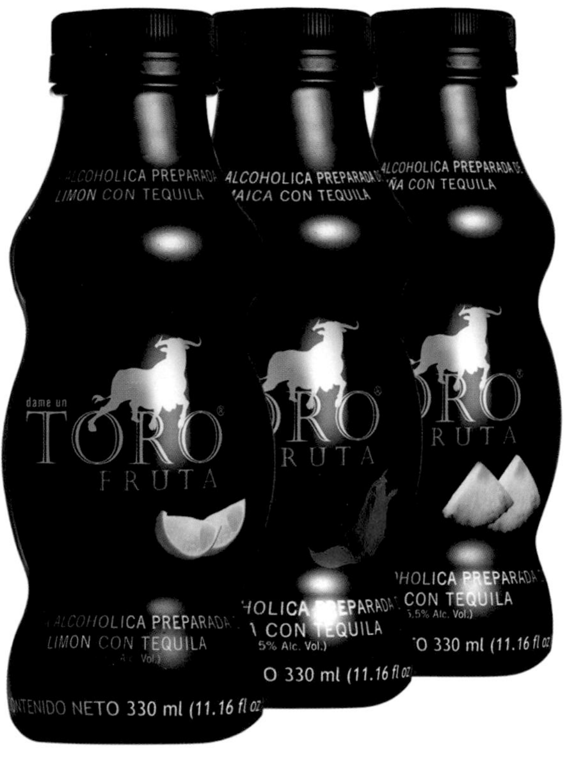

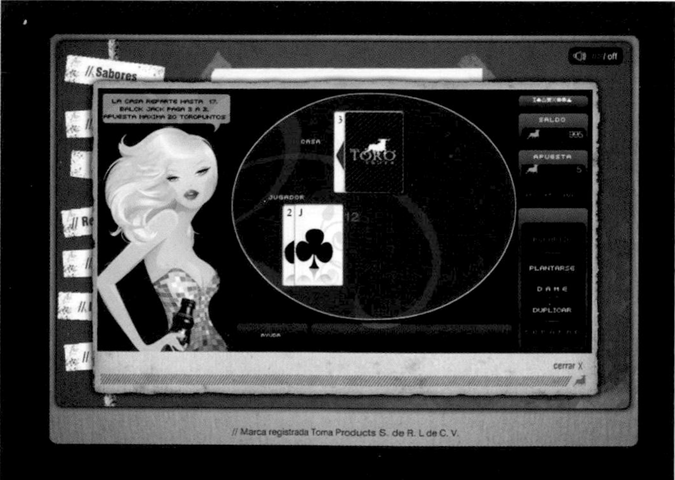

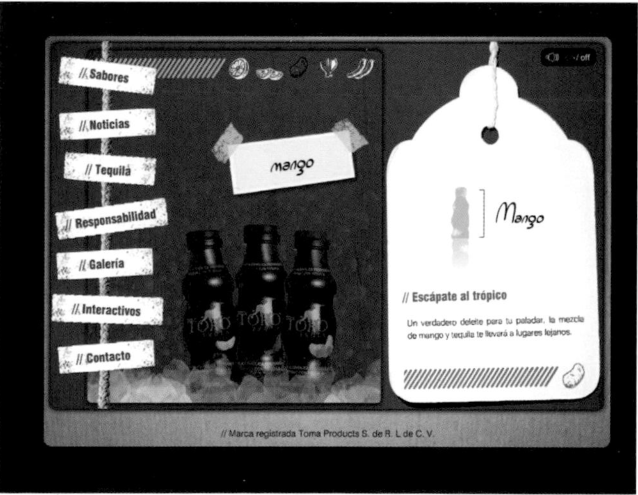

Design Firm: Euphorianet
Location: Monterrey, N.L., Mexico
Client: Toma Products
Industry: Food & Beverage

Design Firm: Watt International
Location: Toronto, Ont. Canada
Client: Cineplex Entertainment
Industry: Environmental Design

6
6
5
5
4
3
2
2
1
1

Hotel Renew

What is now Hotel Renew was once an out-of-date hotel on Waikiki Beach, Hawaii.

When Napili Partners, a California-based investment group, spotted the pedestrian Ocean Tower Hotel in 2005, it struck them as a real estate opportunity ready for the taking. They re-imagined the hotel as a destination for a luxury-seeking, international clientele: business travelers, eastbound Asians, Europeans and other affluent Generation X-type travelers looking for a sophisticated boutique hotel experience.

Napili Partners hired Honolulu designer John Wingard of John Wingard Design to create a brand package in harmony with the hotel's repositioning. With the basic color scheme already in place, San Francisco-based interior designer Juin Ho used his environmentally conscious, Euro-Pacific vision to handle all the décor decisions, designing everything from the 72 guest rooms to the staff's uniforms.

Wingard began the branding for the newly rechristened Hotel Renew with a relaxed but urbane wordmark that evoked the sensibilities of Gropius and Le Corbusier. In fact, Wingard used lowercase Bauhaus, a type inspired by the famous interwar atelier. He also lowered the ascending strokes of the *h* and *l* in *hotel* and rotated the *e*.

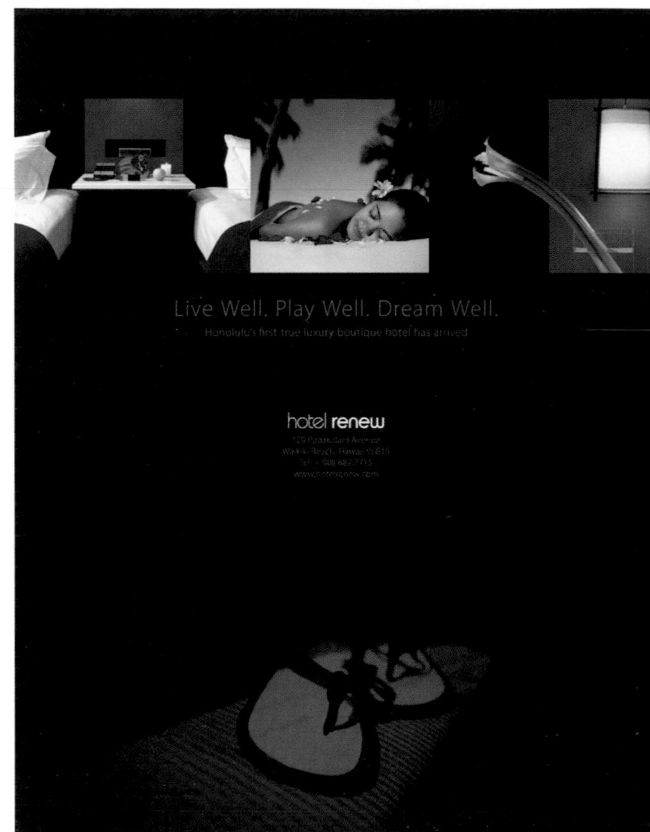

Design Firm: John Wingard Design
Location: Honolulu, Hawaii
Client: Napili Partners
Industry: Hotel & Resort

hotel renew

With input from the hotel team, Wingard designed the Web site to bring the hotel's feel online. In addition to the things mentioned above, John Wingard Design also delivered signage and in-room materials to complete the elegantly modern feel of this completely remodeled hotel. Best of all, they left the kitschy Hawaiiana behind in the past where it belonged.

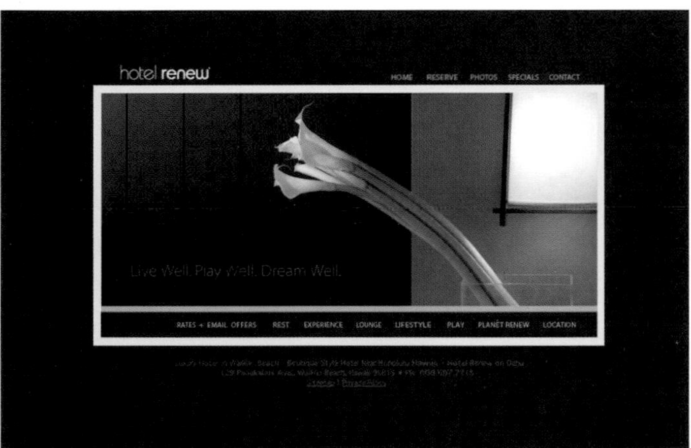

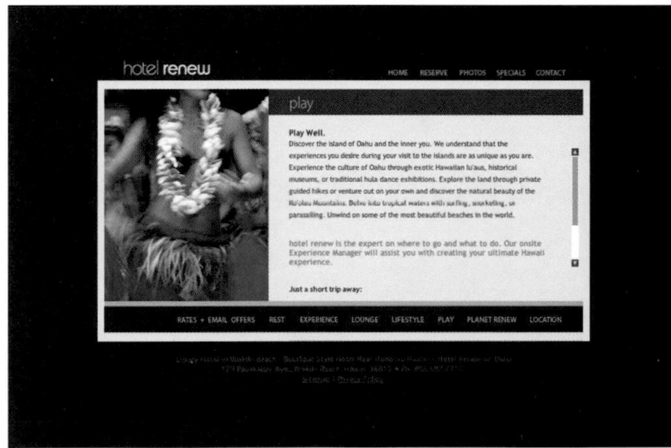

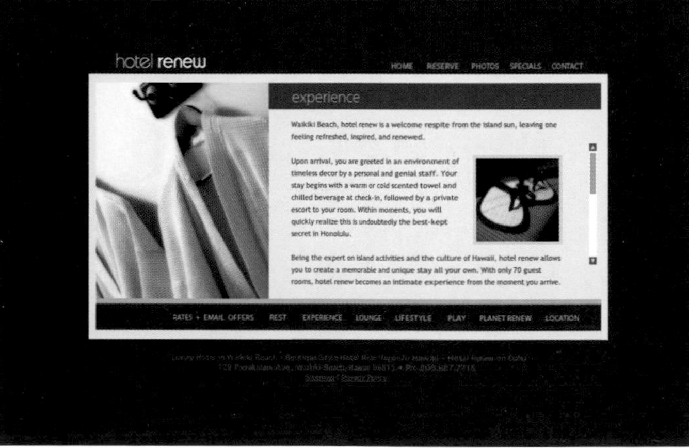

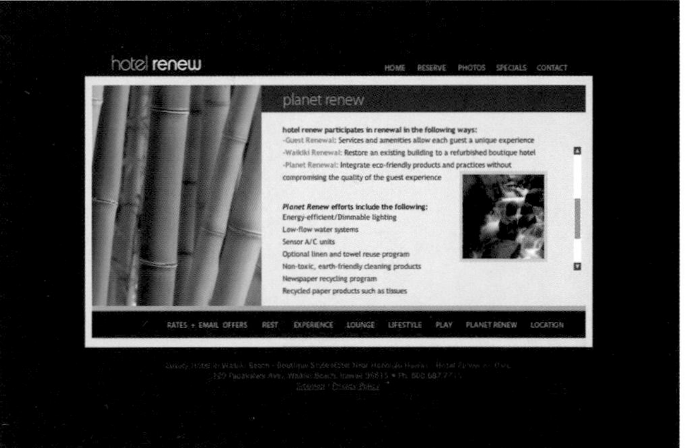

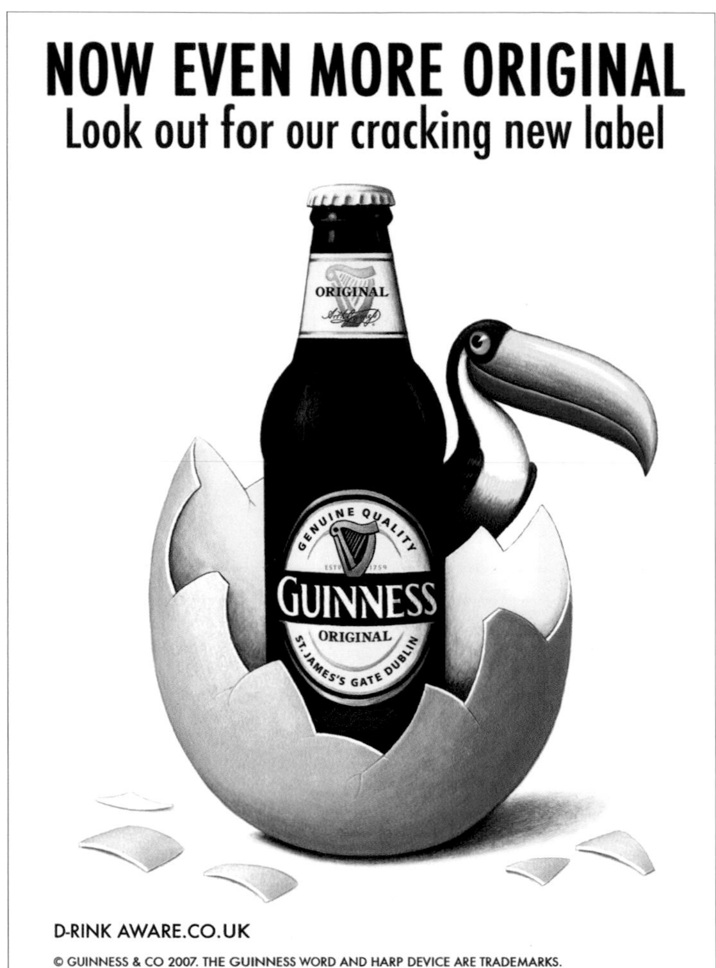

Design Firm: **James Marsh Design**
Location: Hythe, Kent, United Kingdom
Client: Guinness & Co.
Industry: Beverage

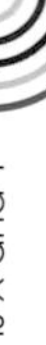

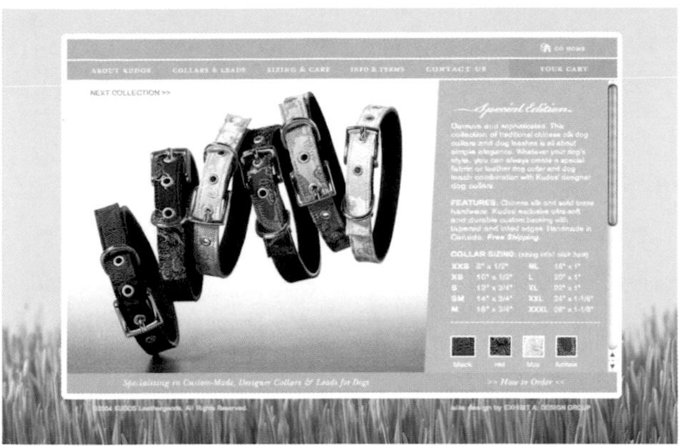

Design Firm: Exhibit A: Design Group
Location: Vancouver, B.C., Canada
Client: Kudos Leathergoods
Industry: Pet Care

Back

Front

Design Firm: Goldforest
Location: Hollywood, Fla.
Client: Continuum Sales & Marketing Corp.
Industry: Housewares

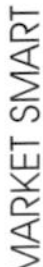

VOLVO C30

Design Firm: Euphorianet
Location: Monterrey, N.L., Mexico
Client: Volvo Bil Monterrey
Industry: Automotive

Design Firm: element3media
Location: Phoenix, Ariz.
Client: element3media/angel society
Industry: Nonprofit/Education

Design Firm: Ian Lynam Design
Location: Tokyo, Japan
Client: Kastner & Partners/Red Bull
Industry: Sports, Food, Beverage

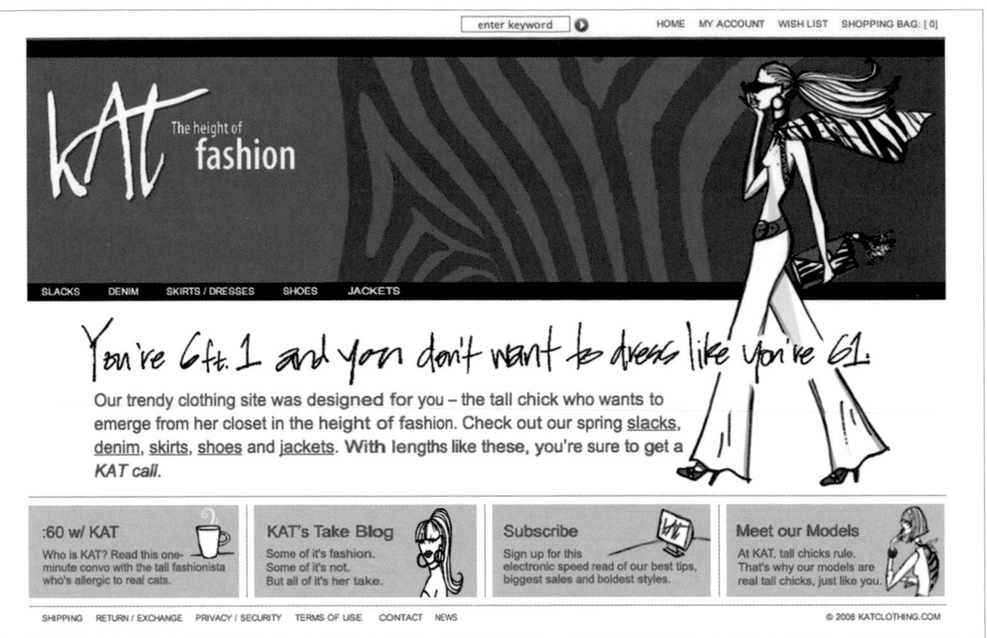

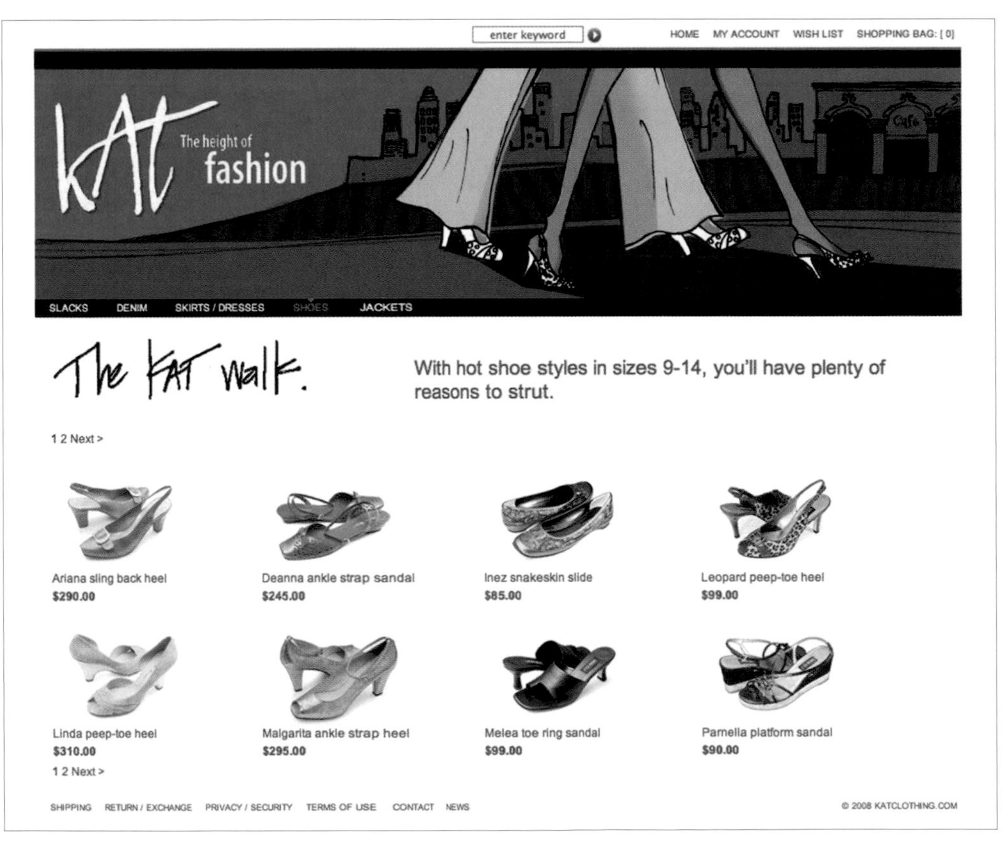

Design Firm: Miller Meiers Design for Communication
Location: Lawrence, KS.
Client: KAT Clothing
Industry: Fashion

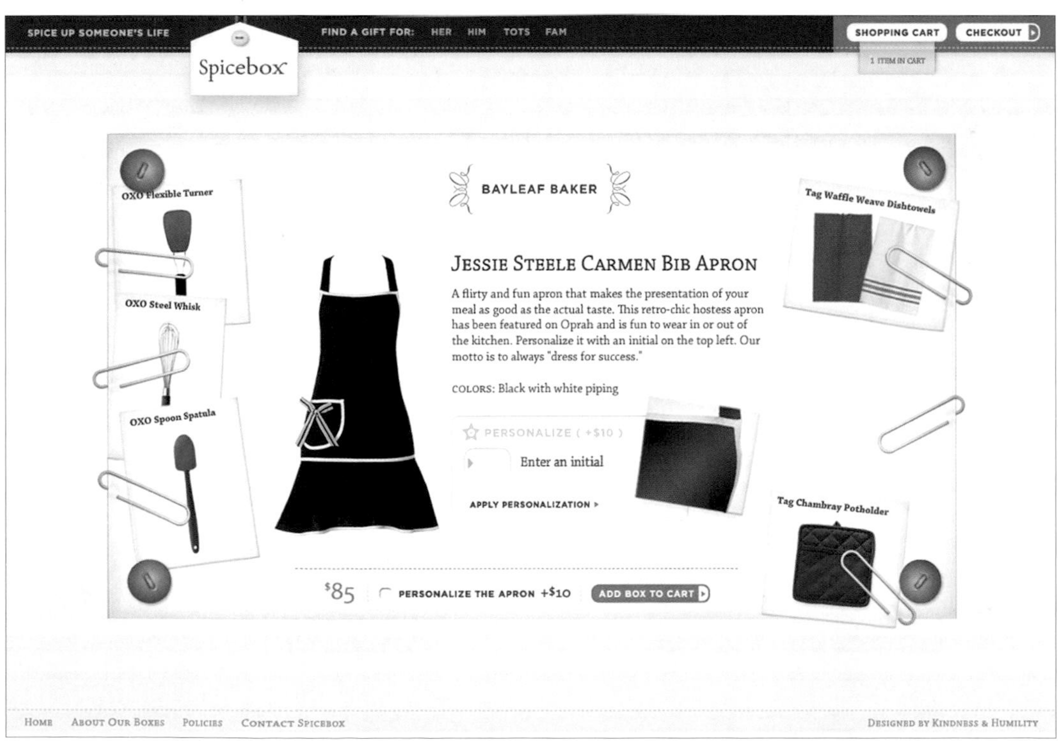

Design Firm: Parliament
Location: Portland, Ore.
Client: Spicebox
Industry: Novelty Gifts

Design Firm: JGA
Location: Southfield, Mich.
Client: Lenox Group Inc.
Industry: Retail

delight
enjoy
decorate
living artfully

Design Firm: Velocity
Location: Boston, Mass.
Client: Pixelfun
Industry: Photography

Design Firm: Velocity
Location: Boston, Mass.
Client: Edward Carriere
Industry: Retail

On Paper
GRADUATE
M.F.A.
JUNIOR DESIGNER
HEAD DESIGNER
CREATIVE DIRECTOR
STARTED OWN LINE
E-COMMERCE QUEEN
SNOWBOARDER

In Life
ROCKSTAR.

Irwin Union Bank
IrwinUnion.com
650 Town Center Dr. | Suite 150 | Costa Mesa | 714.850.6440

Design Firm: FACET Creative and Jenifer Tracy Designs
Location: Los Angeles, Calif.
Client: Irwin Union Bank
Industry: Finance/Banking

Design Firm: Baer Design Group
Location: Evanston, Ill.
Client: Lazy Days Tea
Industry: Food & Beverage

Design Firm: SUPERBIG Creative
Location: Seattle, Wash.
Client: Jones Soda
Industry: Food & Beverage

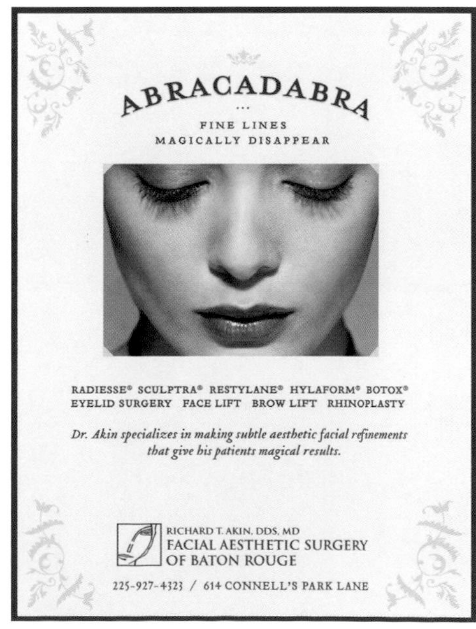

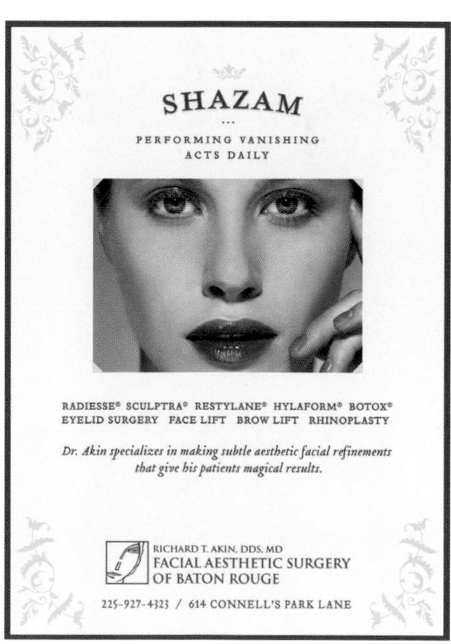

Design Firm: BBR Creative
Location: Lafayette, La.
Client: Dr. Akin
Industry: Medical

Design Firm: Exhibit A: Design Group
Location: Vancouver, B.C., Canada
Client: Sapadilla Soap Co.
Industry: Home Cleaning

Design Firm: Turner Duckworth
Location: San Francisco, CA. and London, England
Client: Schwarzkopf
Industry: Haircare

Design Firm: BIRD
Location: Hollywood, Calif.
Client: Speed
Industry: Entertainment/Broadcast Cable

Design Firm: Anderson Design Group
Location: Nashville, TN
Client: Mercury Records
Industry: Music

Design Firm: Turner Duckworth
Location: San Francisco, CA. and London, England
Client: The Coca-Cola Co.
Industry: Food & Beverage

Design Firm: Wallace Church Inc.
Location: New York, N.Y.
Client: Dial Corporation
Industry: Health & Beauty

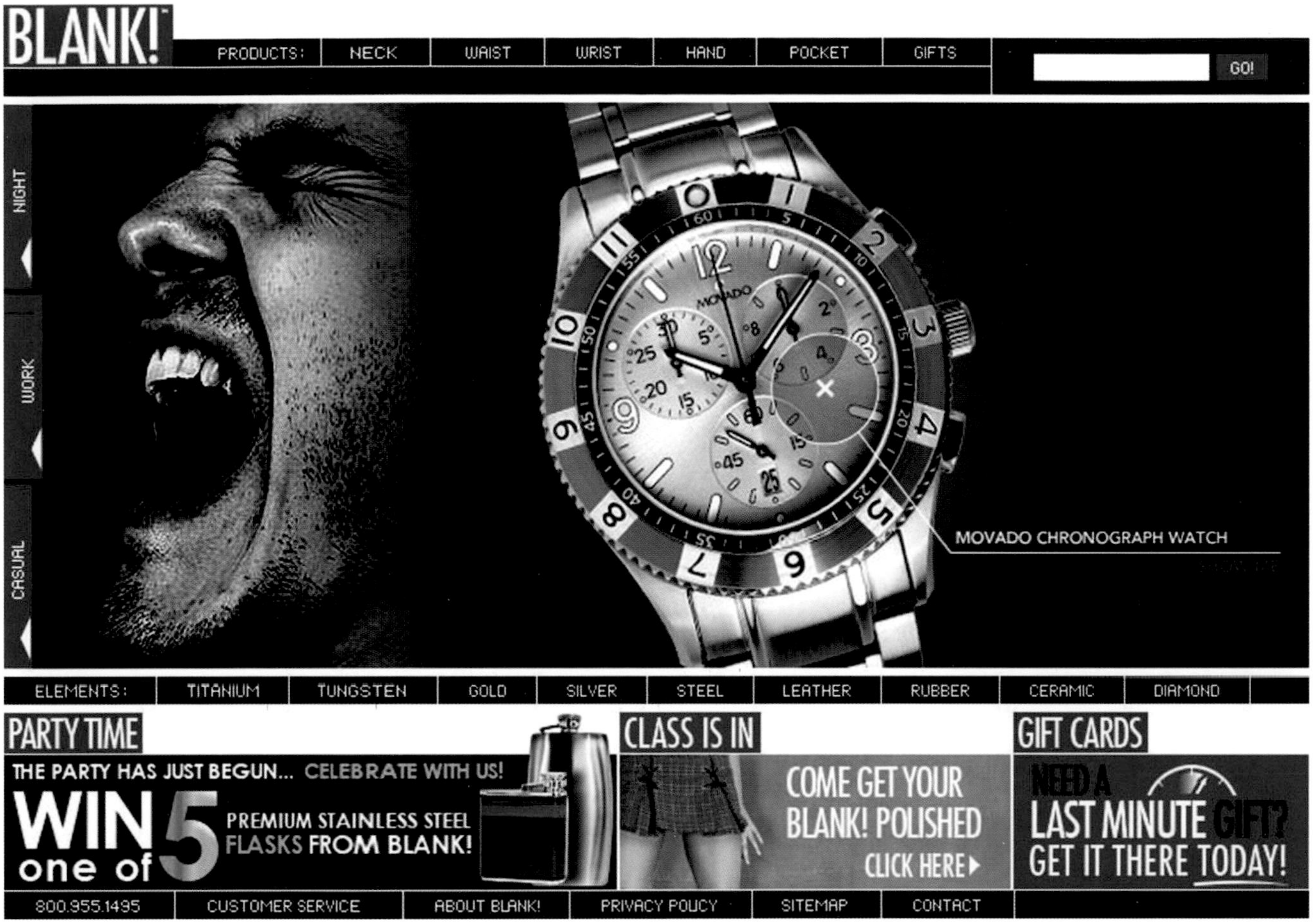
BLANK!
PRODUCTS: NECK WAIST WRIST HAND POCKET GIFTS
GO!
NIGHT
WORK
CASUAL
MOVADO CHRONOGRAPH WATCH
ELEMENTS: TITANIUM TUNGSTEN GOLD SILVER STEEL LEATHER RUBBER CERAMIC DIAMOND
PARTY TIME
THE PARTY HAS JUST BEGUN... CELEBRATE WITH US!
WIN one of 5 PREMIUM STAINLESS STEEL FLASKS FROM BLANK!
CLASS IS IN
COME GET YOUR BLANK! POLISHED
CLICK HERE
GIFT CARDS
NEED A LAST MINUTE GIFT?
GET IT THERE TODAY!
800.955.1495 CUSTOMER SERVICE ABOUT BLANK! PRIVACY POLICY SITEMAP CONTACT

Design Firm: Kurani
Location: Red Bank, N.J.
Client: BLANK! Company LLC
Industry: Watch & Jewelry

NO ANNUAL CONTRACT
INSTANT MESSAGING
E-MAIL TEXT MESSAGING
QUICK START UP
ogo
AT&T Wireless

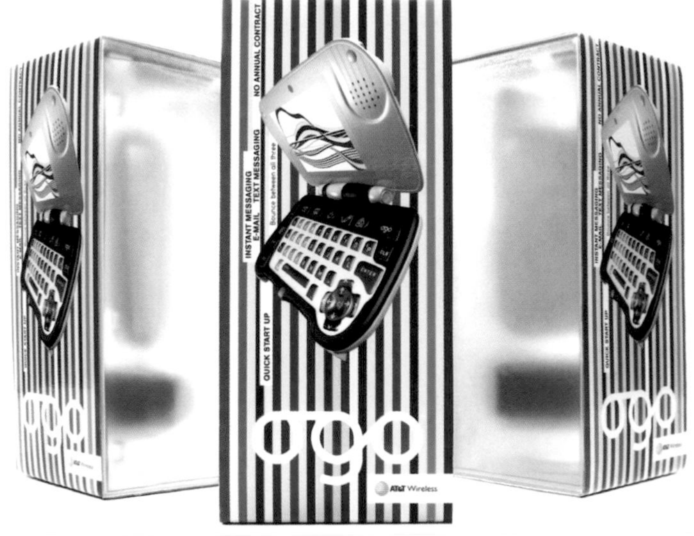

Design Firm: COLLINS
Location: New York, NY
Client: AT&T Wireless
Industry: Mobile Communication

Intercontinental Breakfast

Kellogg's may be the first name in breakfast food, but marketing decades-old mascots as an international lifestyle brand required a balance of classic iconography and current graphic trends. That's why Brand Central, Kellogg's brand strategy firm, approached GelComm, a design company in Glendale, Calif., to expand the Kellogg's presence among Generations X and Y. "They chose us because of our experience with licensing and product development," says owner Patricio Fuentes. The resulting product lines, Daydream Sketch and Kidult (for kids to tweens) and Vantage Vintage and Around the World (for the teen-to-young adult market), tapped into a nostalgia both actual and yet unrealized.

"Kellogg's came to us needing a new point of view, so people would feel something new and interesting," says senior designer Alicia Lichens. "They gave us license to shake it up a bit, but we worked very closely with them." Treading the fine line between updating and completely changing the image of such familiar characters as Tony the Tiger and Toucan Sam, says creative director Patrick Raske, involved close collaboration. "We had to build the relationship and that trust," he says. "It was a lot of give and take, respecting the legal [image] while creating new art." Adds Lichens: "They trusted us and we gently massaged the character art. We weren't going to take it too far, but we *were* going to push it. It worked out great."

The expansion of the Kellogg's brand into kitchen goods, home items such as pillows, breakfast-oriented ceramics and apparel was "a unique challenge for us," says Raske. "With Kidults, we had an opportunity to completely redraw the character art." Still, adds Lichens, they couldn't stray too far. "One imperative was to work with the vintage art," she says.

Design Firm: GelComm
Location: Glendale, Calif.
Client: Kellogg's
Industry: Consumer Products

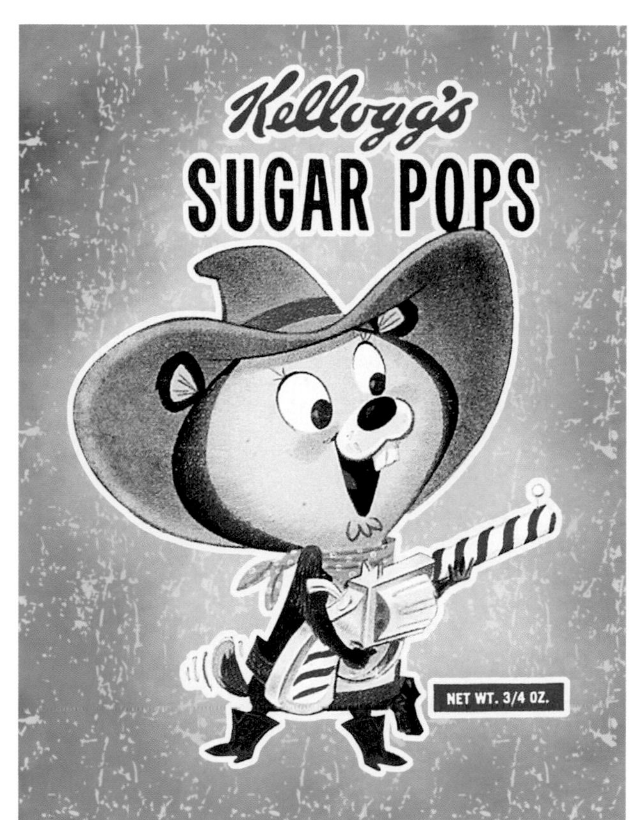

For the Around the World line, products feature non-English writing, often with several languages on one item. "We understand the international representation," says Lichens, "so we presented the trend with a unique twist." Raske was "enchanted with the idea of taking something very American and putting a twist on it—something familiar with something translated." To that end, Lichens and Raske looked no further than their own office. "We have a great international group of designers so we had access to good translations, from Tagalog to Japanese, Spanish to Mandarin, Hindi," notes Lichens, "but with a fun and unique twist. 'L'Eggo my Eggo' became 'Let go of my Eggo.' Instead of 'Have a good breakfast,' sometimes it was 'Have a happy breakfast.'"

"At the end of the day we loved the rooster–rising sun–sunny optimism," adds Raske, alluding to the iconic Kellogg's Corn Flakes mascot—a symbol that inspired an even earlier generation: John Lennon wrote *Sgt. Pepper's* "Good Morning Good Morning" for the Beatles after eyeing the bird on a cereal ad. But, of course, one generation's nostalgia doesn't fit all; while Generation X may have grown up on Saturday morning cartoons with a bowl of Apple Jacks, younger consumers raised on lattes for breakfast may have no such inborn affection for their parents' (or grand-parents') characters. "Our nostalgia is not everyone's," says Raske. "These programs have a good fringe overlap—[people in their] mid-to-late thirties buying products for their children. How do we make this relevant to a younger demographic which doesn't have this built-in history? That's what makes it really exciting. We're going to see these products for a long, long time."

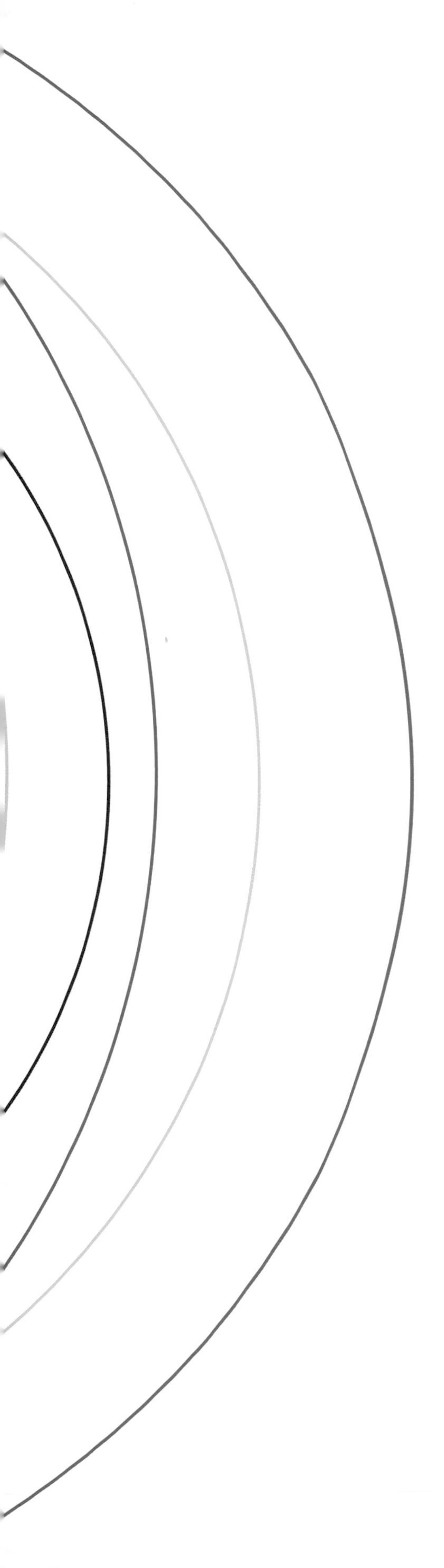

Baby Boomers

Introduction by Jim Gilmartin

As the adult median age rises higher than ever, pressure is building on marketing and sales professionals to learn how to better market to a dominantly older consumer population (the "Boomer+ Customer Majority"). Progress in this direction must be founded in the recognition that young, middle-aged and old minds all work differently. Few marketers have enough working knowledge of the worldviews, values, needs and motivations of people in so-called Second Half markets to be as effective in those markets as they have been in First Half markets. Lack of market research is likely the main reason for this.

A survey conducted by *Active Times* reported that people over age 50 feel that advertising messages geared to them are condescending, stereotypical and place far too much emphasis on medical conditions. Smart marketers are replacing conventional approaches with new ways of understanding and connecting with mature Americans, as chronological age is no longer considered sufficient for understanding older adults. Midlife developmental changes in the behavior of members of the Boomer+ Customer Majority challenge the view of marketing as a game of persuasion. The object of marketing has been to "capture" customers and overwhelm their wills, and with this market, that's why so much

A survey conducted by Active Times reported that people over age 50 feel that advertising messages geared to them are condescending, stereotypical and place far too much emphasis on medical conditions.

Jim Gilmartin has emerged as one of America's experts on communicating, marketing and sales to baby boomer and older consumers. He established Wheaton, Ill.-based *Coming of Age Inc.* in 1991 as a full-service integrated marketing/advertising firm focused upon helping clients develop profitable strategies for baby boomer and older consumer markets. The author of numerous articles, Jim is a frequent speaker at professional conferences, and is also one of the founders of *The Society for Maturing Consumer Marketing*, a national think tank that meets twice a year to discuss the latest research and trends in the field. *www.comingofage.com*

marketing fails. Adaptive marketing can put marketing back on track, making customers co-creators of marketing success. Customers provide energy to move marketing forward at a faster clip than the marketer can achieve alone.

One of the major points to remember is that you sell nothing directly to the conscious intellect. This is so very important and the number one reason why so many advertisements and sales letters fail to produce results. It's a proven fact that human beings make buying decisions on an emotional basis—no matter how much we analyze it afterward to reassure ourselves we made the right choice. Research has shown that consumers' final decisions are not the direct product of the reasoning process; in fact, emotions drive boomers and older consumers in their purchase decisions. The reasoning process will confirm their decisions, but it doesn't start there.

Let's look at emotions from the marketers' perspective. Do you use emotional marketing techniques in your advertising right now? If you're not, then you're losing possible sales and profits. The next time you see a television commercial, stop and look at it from an advertiser's standpoint. These companies are paying millions of dollars for advertising that works by relating to their target markets by appealing to their emotions and helping them visualize themselves owning that particular product or service. (Why else would people spend twice as much to buy a particular house or car when the lower priced version would fill the need?) Advertisers know this—and that's why the luxury business is booming. But how do we do this in an advertisement or in personal selling, package design, branding and training of salespeople?

One of the major points to remember is that you sell nothing directly to the conscious intellect. This is so very important and the number one reason why so many advertisements and sales letters fail to produce results.

Ads and sales approaches should be should be easy to read and experiential in nature. They should reflect empathy for the values of this demographic in terms of your company's products and services being a gateway to desired experiences of the targets. Above all, remember: Don't focus on selling the product. Instead focus on selling your knowledge of the customers' needs and how your product ultimately can help them reach their goals and wants.

At 78 million in number spending $2 trillion—or 70 percent of the United States' net worth in 28 percent of the population—each year, baby boomers are the largest and wealthiest demographic segment of the population today.[16]

Baby boomers continue to embrace the Internet, with 83.2 percent online in 2011, up from 75 percent in 2006.[17]

Because of health and science advances and their own state of mind, baby boomers don't consider themselves "old" by any means—they define "old age" as beginning at age 85, when in fact their own life expectancy is 82.3.[18]

At least 50 percent of baby boomers at every income level are likely to choose brands that are environmentally safe. When it comes to advertising, "green boomers" (the 40 million baby boomers who choose environmentally safe brands) are "seeking authenticity and relevance, as well as real information about products."[19]

Adults 45 and older are poised to outspend younger adults by $1 trillion a year starting in 2010.[20]

Basic Facts About: Baby Boomers

Rules to follow when Marketing to Baby Boomers:

1. **They're different and they know it.**
Often marketers put all those born between 1946 and 1964 in the same category. They assume these baby boomers look, act and think alike. Although they have common human traits, values and motivations, they have vast differences in their thinking and actions.

2. **How they think is as important as what they think.**
Creators of product messages need to become intimately familiar with the so-called "hidden drivers" of consumers' behavior than do the consumers themselves. These drivers tend to be stage-of-life specific.

3. **Purchase motivations do not originate in the conscious mind.** The finding that people process hypothetical information differently than they do real-life information justifies the recent trend toward studying consumers in their natural living and shopping environments.

4. **As midlife (40+) approaches, people tend to respond increasingly to emotional stimuli.** The older a market, the more effective it is for an advertiser to present a product in story form. To arouse the strongest attention, product messages should be rich in sensory stimuli. Even though the right brain can't process words, any storyteller can tell you that words can create sensory images.

5. **Initial determination of information relevance occurs unconsciously.** When a person sees an ad, the right brain initially determines if the ad has personal relevance. The right brain conducts a process called information triage to disseminate information flow to the conscious mind, with the primary criterion being relevance to a person's interests. Creating product messages that survive information triage is the biggest challenge in marketing. When a message has relevance to a person's interest, the right brain will take note. Unfortunately, many communications that draw the viewer, listener or reader into an emotional scene too abruptly cut to product information. Deep inside the brain, this action causes trouble. The right hemisphere is still highly active, making it difficult for the brain to process words. In short, the timing can muddle the message.

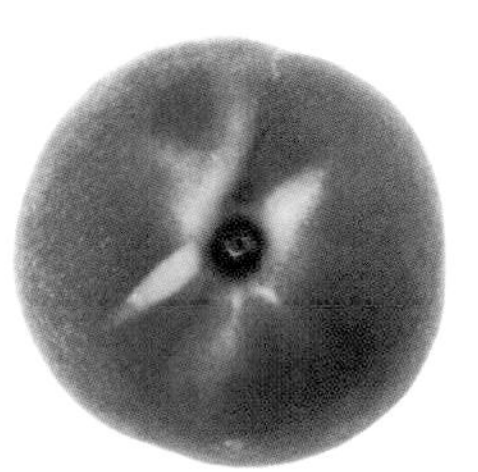

What's your *breakfast* got to do with breast cancer?

Did you know that only 1 in 10 women who have breast cancer have a genetic history of the disease? Pure choices, like eating organic, natural foods, can make a difference. To get the facts about the environmental causes of breast cancer and learn simple ways you can ask, act and live to reduce your risk, visit www.pureprevention.org.

What's your *make-up* got to do with breast cancer?

Did you know that only 1 in 10 women who have breast cancer have a genetic history of the disease? Pure choices, like using natural, safe cosmetics, can make a difference. To get the facts about the environmental causes of breast cancer and learn simple ways you can ask, act and live to reduce your risk, visit www.pureprevention.org.

Design Firm: BBMG
Location: New York, N.Y.
Client: Breast Cancer Fund and LUNA Bar
Industry: Nonprofit

Design Firm: Minelli, Inc.
Location: Boston, Mass.
Client: Rose Fitzgerald Kennedy Greenway Conservancy
Industry: Nonprofit, Land Conservancy

Contact Us | Submit A Business Plan

FLYBRIDGE
CAPITAL PARTNERS

ABOUT US | TEAM | PORTFOLIO | RESOURCES | NEWS & EVENTS | BLOG

JEFFREY BUSSGANG, GENERAL PARTNER

Jeff is a General Partner at Flybridge Capital Partners whose investment interests and entrepreneurial experience are in consumer, Internet commerce, marketing services, software and wireless start-ups.

Jeff currently represents the firm on the boards of BzzAgent, Click Tactics, go2 Media, i4cp, InnerWireless, Mall Networks, SimpleTuition, and Transpera and was previously a director at Brontes Technologies (acquired by 3M) and PanGo Networks (merged with InnerWireless).

Jeff's popular blog on helping demystify the venture business for entrepreneurs, "Seeing Both Sides", can be found at www.bostonvcblog.com.

Background
Prior to joining the firm in January 2003, Jeff co-founded Upromise (acquired by Sallie Mae), a loyalty marketing and financial services firm that currently manages $20 billion in college savings assets, where he served as President, Chief Operating Officer and Board Director. Prior to Upromise, Jeff was an executive at Open Market, an Internet commerce software leader that went public in 1996 and grew to nearly $100 million in revenues. During his five-year tenure, he served as Vice President of Worldwide Marketing and Business Development, Vice President of Worldwide Professional Services and head of Product Management. Prior to Open Market, Jeff was with the strategy consulting firm, The Boston Consulting Group, and served on the executive team of Athena Design, an object-oriented software start-up. Jeff was named to the Boston Business Journal's "40 under 40" list in 2006.

Education
Jeff holds a BA in Computer Science from Harvard University where he graduated magna cum

David Aronoff
Jeff Bussgang
Kate Castle
Anand Daniel
Michael Greeley
Chip Hazard
Jon Karlen
Bruce Revzin

© 2008 FLYBRIDGE CAPITAL PARTNERS 500 Boylston Street, 18th floor Boston, Massachusetts 02116 Ph: 617-307-9270 Fx: 617-307-9293

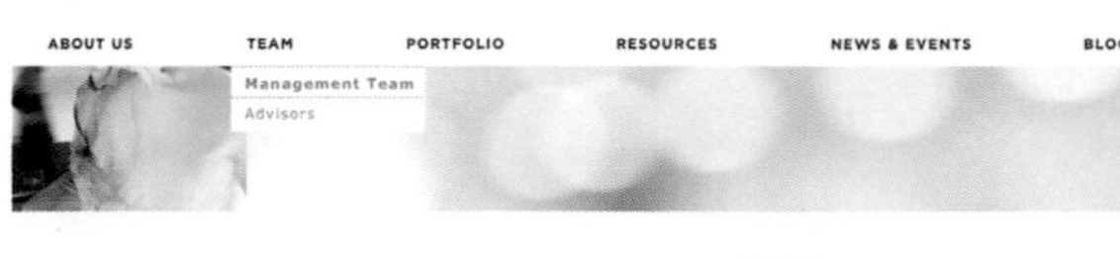

Flybridge Capital Partners is led by five general partners with more than a half century of combined investment and operational experience across the consumer, healthcare, and information technology markets.

Our first-hand knowledge of the products, technologies and markets we invest in enables us to provide entrepreneurs and CEOs with guidance and support throughout all the stages of growth.

Our open, candid style provides the basis for the strong relationships and partnerships we build with entrepreneurs. We are passionate about the companies and markets we invest in and strive to be approachable, innovative, thoughtful, and committed investors who work hard on behalf of our entrepreneurs.

JEFF BUSSGANG, GENERAL PARTNER

© 2008 FLYBRIDGE CAPITAL PARTNERS 500 Boylston Street, 18th floor Boston, Massachusetts 021-6 Ph: 617-307-9270 Fx: 617-307-9293

Design Firm: Minelli, Inc.
Location: Boston, Mass.
Client: Flybridge Capital Partners
Industry: Venture Capitalist

The Rockwood

Boutique Retirement Living
330 West Lockwood Ave.
Webster Groves, MO 63119
Telephone: 314-963-0029

Home
Our History
Services
Amenities
Floor Plans
The Neighborhood
Frequently Asked Questions
Newsletter
Open House & Special Events
Contact

Text Size
A A A

The *Active Lifestyle* you Deserve in the *Neighborhood You Love.* SM

Welcome to The Rockwood

.......for active adults age 62 or better who love tree-lined streets, sidewalk cafes and nearby shops. Located in the heart of Historic Old Webster, The Rockwood brings exceptional retirement living to one of St. Louis' finest neighborhoods.

You'll love the convenience of The Rockwood retirement community where you really are steps away from shops, restaurants, banking and more. While our location is outstanding, it's our Style and Service that set us apart. The Rockwood's apartment homes and amenities have elegant style with the charm of yesterday and all the comforts of today. And our personalized Services are second to none.

With just 29 apartments, you get to know your neighbors and our staff will deliver services that meet your individual needs. At The Rockwood, our days revolve around your schedule not ours.

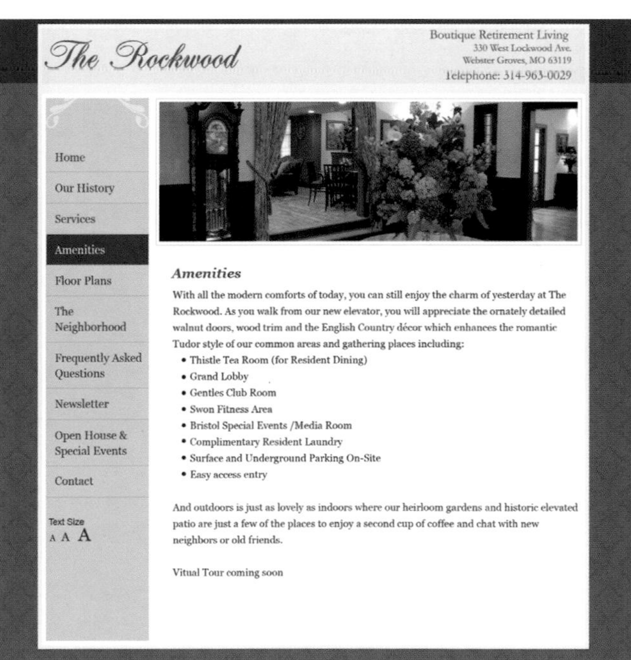

Design Firm: Indigo Image
Location: Wildwood, Mo.
Client: The Rockwood
Industry: Senior Living Community

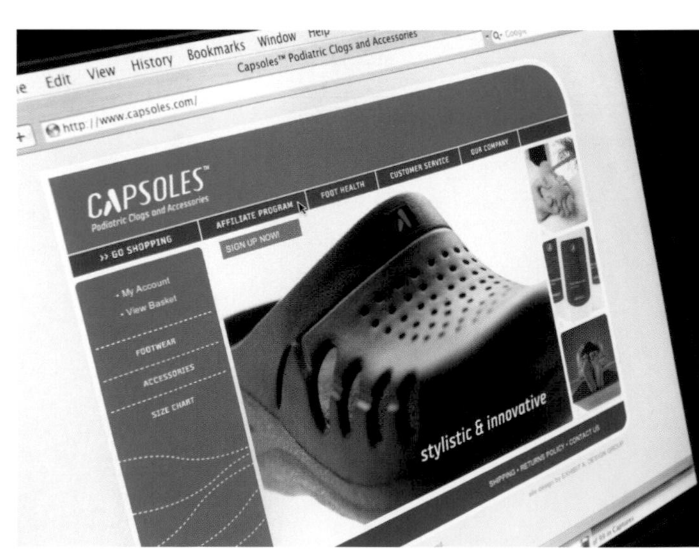

Design Firm: Exhibit A: Design Group
Location: Vancouver, B.C., Canada
Client: Capsoles
Industry: Podiatric Clogs

Design Firm: Morgan_Mohon
Location: Fredricksburg, Texas
Client: Skywater
Industry: Real Estate

N
PRIVATE FLIGHT HOME

W
EAGLE ON #14

E
BURGERS AT THE CLUB

yourTexas

S
ROUNDS WITH DAD

Your best drives come with commanding views. With Lake LBJ and Horseshoe Bay at hand, you will soon experience our new Jack Nicklaus Signature Golf Course—where heroes are made.

SKYWATER™
OVER HORSESHOE BAY

Skywater. Discover your Texas in every direction.

skywatertexas.com | 866.310.6702

HILL COUNTRY LUXURY HOMES—HOMESITES FROM THE 200s
OPPORTUNITY FOR EXCLUSIVE HORSESHOE BAY RESORT MEMBERSHIP
JACK NICKLAUS SIGNATURE GOLF COURSE UNDER CONSTRUCTION
LEED CERTIFIED APPROACH
PRIVATE JET CENTER, YACHT CLUB & MARINA

A Signature Golf Course

Skywater Over Horseshoe Bay is listed by Skywater Realty—a DMB Realty Company (www.dmbrealty.com).

This promotional information is not an offer in any jurisdiction where prior registration, exemption or qualification requirements have not been met, including, but not limited to, New York, New Jersey and California. Offer void where prohibited or otherwise restricted by law. Prices and planned amenities are based on current proposed development plans that are subject to change without notice. Lot Reservations only may be currently offered in certain neighborhoods. Obtain the Property Report or its equivalent, required by Federal and State law, and read it before signing anything. No Federal or State agency has judged the merits or value, if any, of this property. Warning: CA Dept. of Real Estate has not inspected, examined or qualified this property. © February 2007, HB Texas Development Partners, LP. All rights reserved.

Design Firm: Morgan_Mohon
Location: Fredricksburg, Texas
Client: Skywater
Industry: Real Estate

Design Firm: Franklin Street Marketing
Location: Richmond, Va.
Client: Martin Memorial Health Systems
Industry: Healthcare

Design Firm: Franklin Street Marketing
Location: Richmond, Va.
Client: Martin Memorial Health Systems
Industry: Healthcare

Having a Grand New Time

In discussing the logo for grandparents.com, Markham Cronin of Markham Unlimited in Coral Gables, Fla., challenges the common perception of a homebound, technophobic ancestor. "We'retaking the stigma out of [grandparenting being associated with inactivity]," says the designer, who created the "fun" logo featured prominently on the site. "We're making it fun, interesting and vibrant." He cites a few examples of people who may not strike the general public as being grandparents, but certainly are. "Goldie Hawn is a grandparent," he says. "Goldie Hawn—*wow!* It just boggles the mind."

Cronin chose orange for the principal color because "we wanted to make it very obvious... this wasn't the 'grandparents' you always imagined. We wanted to reframe the definition of 'grandparent.' They're out playing tennis, they're traveling, they're vibrant, they're active. So we have to blow it up and see it in a more modern context."

The most striking—and subtle—feature of the logo is the placement of two faces juxtaposed with each other within the *g*. "We wanted to communicate the visual relationship between grandparents and grandchildren," Cronin says. However, the inspiration didn't come instantly. "It was one of those magical moments in the design process," he says. "We'd done about 60 logos—a lot—and nothing was quite right. Then, I may have been talking on the phone and was doodling, and I drew in faces. I looked down [at the *g*]—there it was! Once we had the solution, it just came together."

The site is "not just for grandparents but grandchildren," says Cronin, who describes his parents as "huge" Internet users. "And parents can get something out of it too. It's an opportunity for a family-based online community that helps the communication between the generations."

"We're taking the stigma out of grandparenting being associated with inactivity."

grandparents.com[SM]
it's great to be grand.

Design Firm: Markham Unlimited
Location: Coral Gables, Fla.
Client: Grandparents.com
Industry: Social Networking

Welcome to
grandparents.com℠
it's great to be grand.
Log In | My Account | My Photos
Choose Font Size
SEARCH
GO
Home
Activities
Travel
Toys & Gifts
Food
Expert Advice
Opinions
Community
FEATURED ARTICLES
That Evil Daughter-in-Law
Getting along is the way to have a healthy relationship with your grandchild. continue
More in Expert Advice
Creating Memories on Horseback
Saddle up for a dude ranch vacation, and get closer ... continue
More in Travel
Loud and Clear
The Philips Digital Baby Monitor offers crystal clear signals ... continue
More in Toys & Gifts
ESSENTIALS
Choose the stage of your GRANDCHILD
Expecting
Baby
Grade Schooler
Tween
Teens +
Staying with daughter and son-in-law when baby arrives
Staying with daughter and son-in-law when baby arrives
Staying with daughter and son-in-law when baby arrives
Staying with daughter and son-in-law when baby arrives
TOP DISCUSSIONS
1. Staying with daughter and son-in-law when baby arrives
Posted by Grandbird on 09/10/07 @ 01:14 AM (9 responses)
2. Calling all Grandparents...I need advice
Posted by mama2mykids on 10/19/07 @ 07:33 PM (5 responses)
3. Looking for a shower gift!
Posted by GrannyRegina on 10/03/07 @ 01:29 PM (4 responses)
4. need advice on dealing with a possessive daughter-in-law
Posted by ladybird on 10/03/07 @ 01:29 PM (2 responses)
101 Things To Do with Your Grandkids
Choose a City
GO
SPONSORED BY PLAYSKOOL
GRANDPARENTS.COM TV
GP-TV
Short Video episodes of "Being Grand"
Baby, It's Cold Outside
It's in the Cards, Part II
Ghoulish Garnish: Decorating for Halloween
GRANDPARENT NEWS
Grandma wrestles gator and saves cat.
Ask the Therapist
My Grandson Is a Picky Eater
The Meaning of No
Lingo Appreciation
Can You Handle Six Weeks With The Grandbaby?
My Daughter-in-Law Is Jealous
Food
15-Minute Meals
Apple Season Recipes
Healthy Drinks for Kids
Video: Making Caramel Apples
At Home
Baby, It's Cold Outside
It's in the Cards, Part II
Ghoulish Garnish: Decorating for Halloween
Things to do. Gifts.
Smart Advice. FREE
Sign up for our newsletter now.
Your email:
SUBSCRIBE
See sample | Privacy Policy
ADVERTISEMENT
Kid Motion
©2007 Hasbro. All Rights Reserved
Believe in Play.
SIMON SAYS SIT 'N SPIN
HONEYBEE HOP
BOUNCE 'N GO INCH-ALONG
TAG TAILS ZOO CHASE
CLICK HERE TO SEE TOYS
PLAYSKOOL
believe in PLAY
Win $5000 for your grandchildren (or anything else important to you)
Enter Our Sweepstakes Now! »
We are giving away piles of toys.
Lorem ipsum dolor sit amet
Enter Now! »
Video Promo Headline goes here.
Lorem ipsum dolor sit amet
Enter Now! »
HELP • TERMS OF SERVICE • ABOUT US • CONTACT US • PRIVACY POLICY • EDITORIAL POLICY • CONTRIBUTE
COMMUNITY GUIDELINES • ADVISORY BOARD • ADVERTISE • COPYRIGHT NOTICES • SUGGESTION BOX • SITE MAP
Copyright © 2007 Grandparents.com LLC, all rights reserved

Design Firm: Philippe Becker
Location: San Francisco, Calif.
Client: Dreamerz
Industry: Pharmaceutical

Design Firm: Miller Meiers Design for Communication
Location: Lawrence, Kan.
Client: Livinity Inc.
Industry: Health & Wellness

AARP.org | AARP Magazine | AARP Bulletin | AARP Segunda Juventud | Discounts & Services | AARP Foundation | AARP en Español | Text Size Options

AARP .ORG

Connect with the AARP Community, it's free.
LOG IN | SIGN UP
Enter Search Terms | SEARCH
Advanced Search

HEALTH | MONEY | LEISURE | CONTRIBUTE | FAMILY | COMMUNITY | MEMBERSHIP

Dream Jobs Lorem Ipsum Dolor

Acupuncture
Release Stress and Live Longer

Dream Jobs Lorem Ipsum Dolor

Dream Jobs Lorem Ipsum Dolor

Healing Pain with Acupuncture

Todays News AARP Bulletin
» Obama Calls for Universal Healthcare
» Lawmakers Seek Social Security Reform
» Workers Who Can't Addord to Retire
More Health News >

AARP MEMBERSHIP
Exclusive Services, Discounts & Social Impact
JOIN NOW Why Join?

AARP Goes local
Find news, events, and people near you
Enter zip code | FIND STUFF

Pill-Free Pain Relief
Learn how this dachshund and other Katrina pets changed national policy. Read More >

No Friend Left Behind
Learn how this dachshund and other Katrina pets changed national policy. Read More >

Most Popular
Most Read | E-mailed | Searched
1. Study Finds Dangers in TV Drug Ads
2. Are You Prepared for Long-Term Care?
3. Legislature 2007: Tax Break Bill
4. Study Finds Dangers in TV Drug Ads
5. Are You Prepared for Long-Term Care?

from the community

Featured Topic
Unlock the longevity secrets of other cultures when you join the AARP Long Lifers group, mentored by aging expert John Doe.

Featured Member
"Let's make this a place where we grandparents can tell the world how much we love our grandchildren."
– Cal Workman
Join the discussion >

More from Community >

Press | Events | Policy & Research | NRTA | Radio
About Us | Contact Us | Jobs | Advertise With Us | Privacy Policy | Terms of Service

Copyright 1995-2007, AARP. All rights reserved

Design Firm: Behavior Design
Location: New York, N.Y.
Client: AARP
Industry: Retirement

Design Firm: Daymon Worldwide Design
Location: Stamford, Conn.
Client: Raley's
Industry: Food & Beverage

Design Firm: Goodman Marketing Partners
Location: San Rafael, Calif.
Client: Avicena Group
Industry: Dermaceuticals

Scientists harness powerful skin care breakthrough.

While conducting research to find ways to improve cellular metabolism and prolong cellular life, scientists discovered a new technology that had amazing **anti-aging benefits for skin**. Patented as Advanced Skin Nourishment™ or ASN™, further research and clinical trials confirmed that this technology delivered critical nourishment to the skin enhancing its ability to regenerate itself. After using products with ASN, skin cells became energized and deeply nourished, providing measurable and visible anti-aging benefits, while renewing skin to a more youthful, radiant appearance.

Now scientists have harnessed the power of ASN in a line of skin care products called Nurigene™. Independent, clinical studies and consumer tests further proved the anti-aging benefits of Nurigene with results that could be felt and seen after only 28-days.

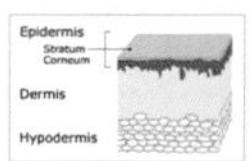

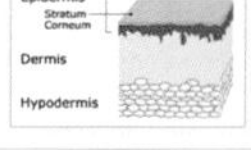

As we age, the skins' ability to perform its function decreases. The stratum corneum becomes thinner, and can no longer effectively act as a barrier to outside elements. The dermis is unable to store a satisfactory level of natural moisture, and collagen and elastin production decreases. Nurigene, with ASN, provides critical nourishment to help deliver fresh, hydrated cells to the skin's surface for a more youthful appearance.

Differences you can ***feel:***
84% felt skin was more hydrated/moisturized

Differences you can ***see:***
91% said skin looked and felt healthier

Differences you ***believe:***
85% claimed skin texture was improved

The secret to healthier, more vibrant skin.

The products in the Nurigene Skin Care Regimen have been specially formulated to work together to remove old skin cells and deliver fresh, hydrated cells to the skin's surface faster. Combined, they support a healthier collagen matrix, and increase the skin's ability to maintain moisture. With regular use, you'll see an improvement in the firmness and elasticity of your skin. In fact, we're so confident you'll see a difference in as little as 28-days, we'll give you a money-back guarantee.*

- A $200 value, now only $144.95!
- Free shipping
- Money-back guarantee

To order: www.nurigene.com/healthy
or call toll free 1-800-669-6199

nurigene™
Advanced Skin Nourishment™

*If you don't see a difference in your skin after 28 days we'll refund your money up to 60 days from the date of purchase. © The Avicena Group, Inc. All rights reserved.

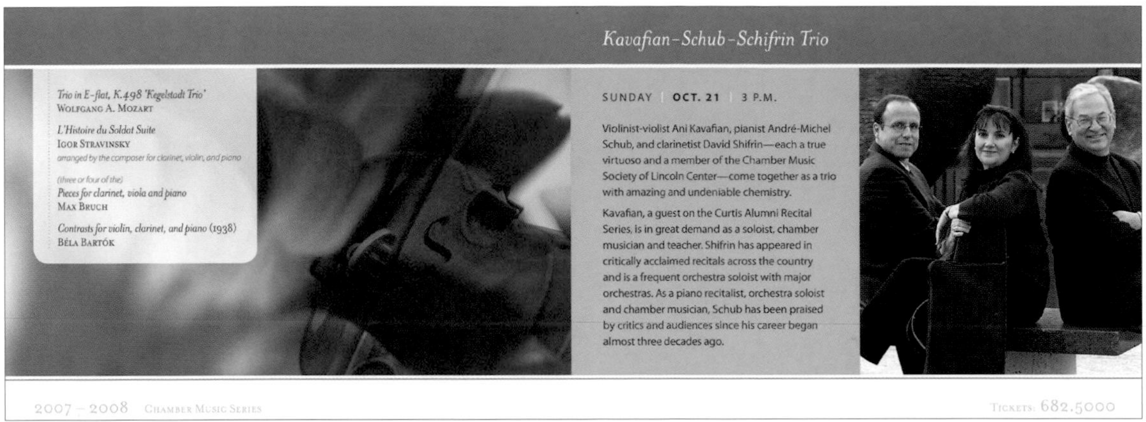

Design Firm: Defteling Design
Location: Portland, Ore.
Client: University of Oregon School of Music
Industry: Nonprofit

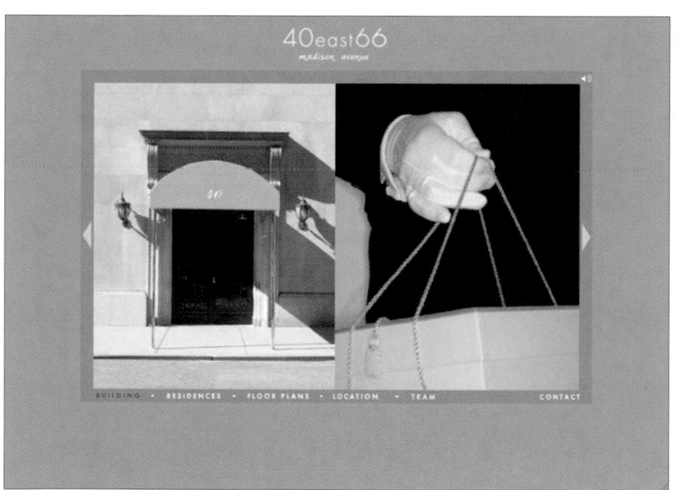

Design Firm: And Partners
Location: New York, N.Y.
Client: 40east66 Madison Avenue
Industry: Real Estate

Design Firm: And Partners
Location: New York, N.Y.
Client: 40east66 Madison Avenue
Industry: Real Estate

Design Firm: Winsper Inc.
Location: Boston, Mass.
Client: MDVIP
Industry: Healthcare

Design Firm: Caliber Group
Location: Tucson, Ariz.
Client: Bogutz & Gordon
Industry: Fiduciary Services

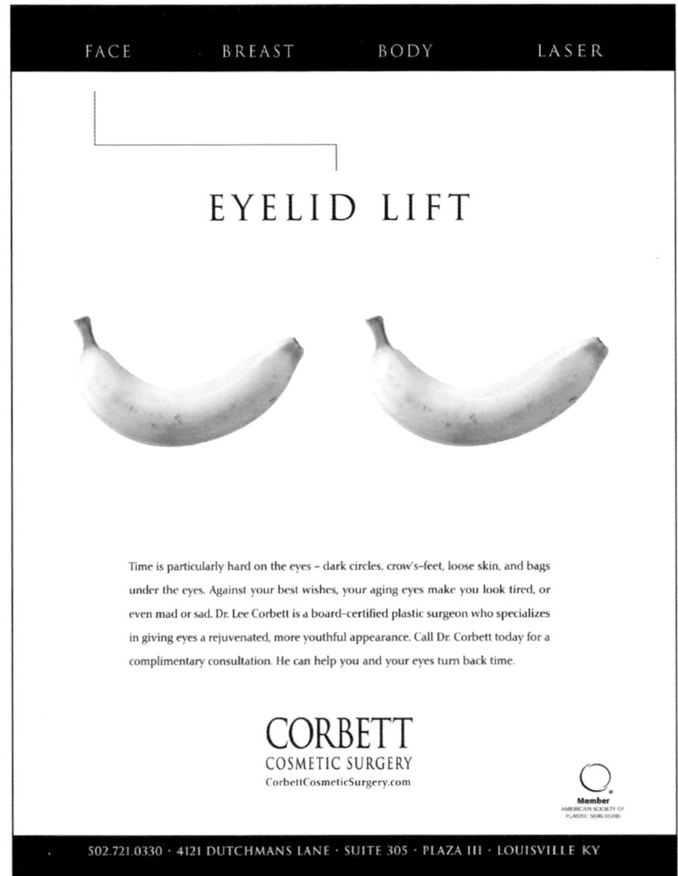

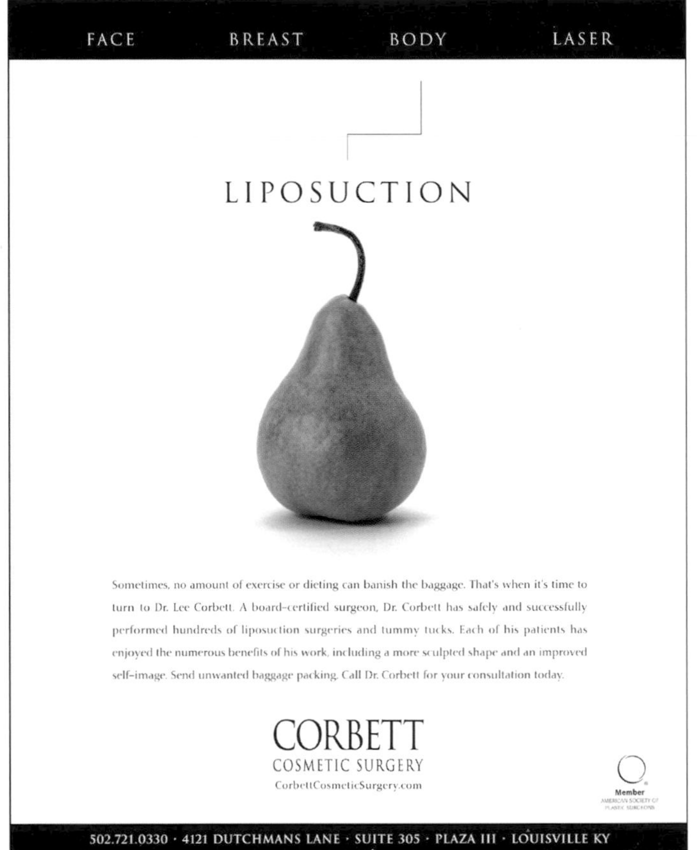

Design Firm: DOGO Communications Inc.
Location: Floyds Knobs, Ind.
Client: Dr. Lee Corbett
Industry: Medical

Design Firm: Winsper Inc.
Location: Boston, Mass.
Client: Exeter Hospital
Industry: Medical

Design Firm: Joni Rae and Associates
Location: Encino, Calif.
Client: NV Perricone LLC
Industry: Health and Beauty

Design Firm: JGA
Location: Southfield, Mich.
Client: Soft Surroundings
Industry: Retail

Design Firm: FACET Creative, Jennifer Tracy Designs
Location: Los Angeles, Calif.
Client: Irwin Union Bank
Industry: Finance/Banking

Design Firm: Essence Design Limited
Location: Birmingham, England
Client: Luxury Vacations UK Limited
Industry: Leisure & Tourism

Turning Over a New Leaf

The white oak is a notoriously long-lived tree, so it only made sense that a community designed for the post-baby boomer set still in the prime of life chose the hardwood for its symbol. "This is not the end!" says Scott Pryor of Pryor Design in Ann Arbor, Michigan.

At White Oak Living, set on 85 acres near Dayton, Ohio, the emphasis is on living—in fact, its slogan is "Inspired Living. Every Day."—and retired couples are its main target. (While single retirees are welcome, it certainly isn't meant to be a haven for the lonely widow or widower to idly while away one's twilight years.) The message, says Pryor, is, "Hey, you're still here, you're still active, join a community comprised of people just like you." And those people, seeking a high-class, elegant living environment, find it in White Oak's "healthy, uplifting lifestyle. It's a very exclusive thing, a Lexus of retirement living." Pryor strived to convey this richness in White Oak's marketing materials, including the Web site—which features boomer couples enjoying such leisure activities as swimming, bicycling and wine tasting—stationery, direct mail pieces and signage at the complex itself.

Like White Oak's residents, the design also is meant to age gracefully. "It's timeless," Pryor says. "We took real care with the color schemes, right down to the primary typeface. Baskerville is timeless, yet romantic." The logo features a metallic copper—an element especially prominent on its printed materials—designed to convey "a lifestyle that's uplifting, with very active retired couples *doing* things. We want to inspire people with a richness and a classic [feeling] contrasted with these very vibrant and active people enjoying really wonderful cuisine and having access to a really wonderful spa." Even though the community resembles more a destination resort than a traditional retirement

WHITE OAK

Design firm: Pryor Design
Location: Ann Arbor, Mich.
Client: White Oak
Industry: Assisted Living

community, Pryor kept the audience ever in his sight when designing for his market. "While the Web site was extremely important, the sales kit is the crown jewel of the campaign. Remember, [this generation] grew up with books!" While avoiding the hard sell, Pryor created a logo with an evocative yet distinctive touch respectful of its target. The *w* and *o* join with a silhouetted white oak to form a little scene of this corner of southwest Ohio. "It's a gorgeous piece of land," he says, adding that the *w* suggests "not just hills but a pathway leading to it." As for the copper halo that is the *o* around the tree, make no mistake about which way it's going. "It's a sunrise, not sunset," Pryor says emphatically. "That [sun] form is obviously something used often—dawn versus dusk—but dawn is more appropriate for this audience."

If each year represents another trip of the earth around the sun, the journey of White Oak's residents may be long but certainly not downhill. "As we get older, we're actually getting younger," Pryor says. "Turning 40 isn't like it was when your father turned 40. [White Oak's residents] aren't sitting around playing bridge—but they may go out and experience a walking trail."

5
Modern Moms & Hip Parents

Pintsize Shoes

Pintsize Shoes is located in an upmarket shopping center in the heart of Northern California's wine country.

The business turned to a retail package and brand identity design firm in nearby Cotati to create an identity and retail environment that would appeal to the area's design-conscious parents. Session Creative developed signage congruent with the town's design review standards as well as point-of-sale and other branded materials.

The wordmark development anchored the campaign. Dennis Derammelaere, the agency's principal and creative director, chose Kerning Unicase, a mix of letters without a complete uppercase or lowercase set, for the typeface. "The font was merely used as a starting point," he explained, "as we had to manipulate every character to become the end result you see.

"Angled cuts were added to the letters, some were removed. The *'i's* were literally dotted. The curves of the *s* and *e* were refined carefully. And the *p* and *t* were created from scratch to match the style and playfulness of the rest of the mark."

The kid-friendly and modern color scheme features stripes throughout the store, on all signage and on business collateral such as gift cards and business cards.

PintSize
★ shoes for kids ★

Design Firm: Session Creative
Location: Cotati, Calif.
Client: Pintsize Shoes
Industry: Children's Shoes

PintSize
★ shoes for kids ★

Pint Size
★ shoes for kids ★

Pint Size
★ shoes for kids ★

Design Firm: Minelli Inc.
Location: Boston, Mass.
Client: OurKidsWin
Industry: Education

Design Firm: Leibold Associates, Inc.
Location: Neenah, WI
Client: Kimberly-Clark
Industry: General Retail

Design Firm: Enhanced Aesthetic
Location: Newport Coast, Calif.
Client: The Nursery Inc.
Industry: Media

Design Firm: Boon Inc.
Location: Chandler, Ariz.
Client: Boon Inc.
Industry: Toys

Design Firm: BBR Creative
Location: Lafayette, La.
Client: Rooms to Grow
Industry: Retail

Design Firm: Exhibit A: Design Group
Location: Vancouver, B.C., Canada
Client: Parade Organics
Industry: Baby Apparel

Design Firm: Designfarm
Location: Takoma Park, Md.
Client: myright2write.com
Industry: Nonprofit

Design Firm: espluga+associates
Location: Barcelona, Spain
Client: Montse Vicens/Sweet bcn
Industry: Kids' Interior Design & Accessories

Design Firm: Brown Communications Group
Location: Regina, Sask., Canada
Client: Cornwall Shopping Centre
Industry: Retail

Design Firm: 72andSunny
Location: El Segundo, Calif.
Client: Bugaboo Inc.
Industry: Strollers

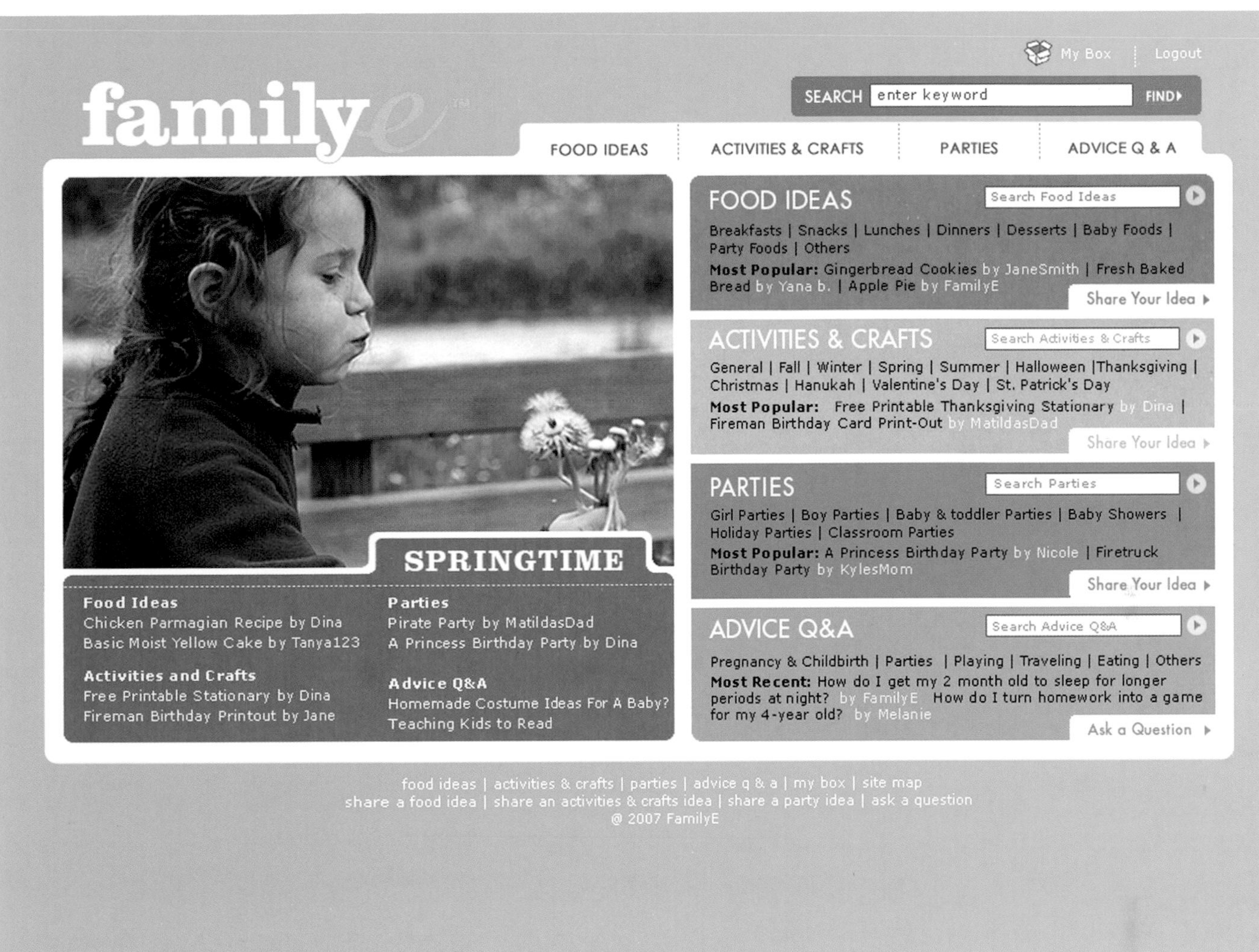

Design Firm: Liquid Pixel Studio
Location: Brooklyn, N.Y.
Client: FamilyE
Industry: Family Entertainment

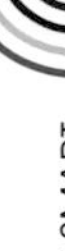

Munchkin

When the management of baby products manufacturer Munchkin Inc. hired CEO and founder of The UXB (The Unexploded Brand), Nancy Jane Goldston, in 2006 for a rebranding campaign, they felt they knew what they were getting. However, UXB raised the brand to unexpected new heights.

Munchkin's CEO felt strongly, for example, about keeping the red in its mark, convinced it had plenty of equity in the color. Goldston, however, sold Munchkin on a distinctive, multicolored logo and branding treatment "to convey the company's vibrancy, character and fusion of modernity."

The equity associated with the old mark remained as UXB kept the traditional red Munchkin heart but playfully rotated the icon 45 degrees and opened the middle.

A heart icon dots the *i* on UXB's redesigned wordmark. The custom type is all rounded lowercase, with strong horizontals. Goldston paid extra attention to the readability of the type, both up close and from a distance. Creative director Glenn Sakamoto modified the *n* and *u* to be inverted mirror images of each other, echoing the curves of the heart logo.

Thanks to the crystal clear direction she got from her client—who told her, "We want to be the Apple of our industry"—Goldston felt empowered to help Munchkin break out of a cluttered pack. She knew an updated brand could reach "the modern mom," as she called the primary target, but also acknowledged the need for Munchkin to be a vibrant brand that aligned with its vision

Design Firm: The UXB
Location: Beverly Hills, Calif.
Client: Munchkin
Industry: Baby Products

of itself as a leader in the development of "unique, timesaving and problem-solving baby care products."

When revamping this brand, UXB not only focused on impressing consumers, but also retailers. Despite having earned a reputation for innovative, award-winning products since its inception in 1991, Munchkin needed more retailers to take greater notice—requiring a much stronger brand energy to overcome fierce competition on the shelf.

To this end, UXB created packaging with an emotional punch. The new packaging, for example, features a baby's face playing peek-a-boo and a new tag line, "It's the Little Things." As Goldston explains, she designed the new look "to convey and reinforce the characteristics of Munchkin as the clever, modern, exciting and fun brand."

UXB integrated every aspect of the brand, with the same colorful tonal boxes on the Web site as on the packaging. The new print ads tied into the look, feel and voice of the brand message on the buyer-friendly Web site and packaging. The end result was a dynamic, coherent package that appealed beautifully to "modern moms," as well as to Munchkin's retail partners.

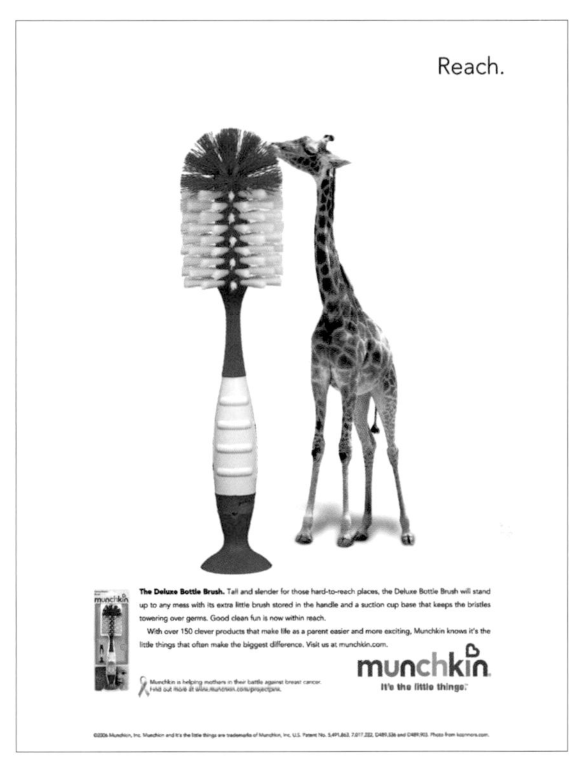

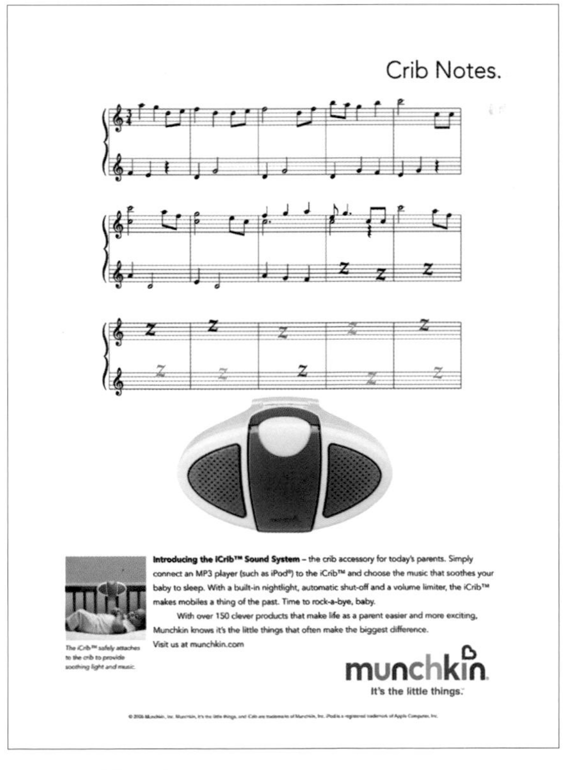

Design Firm: mad studios
Location: Hong Kong, China
Client: babyfirst
Industry: Retail

Design Firm: Local Design Group
Location: St. Paul, Minn.
Client: Go Home Gorgeous
Industry: Health & Wellness

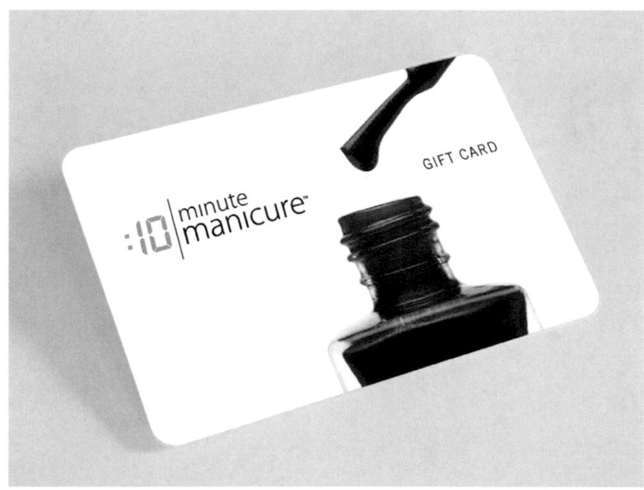

Design Firm: Goldforest
Location: Hollywood, Fla.
Client: 10 Minute Manicure
Industry: Health & Beauty

Design Firm: Netra Nei
Location: Seattle, Wash.
Client: Tiny Bigs
Industry: Children's Accessories

Design Firm: Rock, Paper, Scissors LLC
Location: Lawrenceville, Ga.
Client: Original Belly Works
Industry: Gift

Design Firm: WhiteSpace Creative
Location: Akron, Ohio
Client: Dorel Juvenile Group
Industry: Juvenile Products

Design Firm: FAI Design Group
Location: Irvington, N.Y.
Client: Jamar Labs LLC
Industry: Health & Beauty

Design Firm: Lunarboy
Location: Oakland, Calif.
Client: Gearhead Mom
Industry: Blogs

Design Firm: Sharon Avnon
Location: Brooklyn, N.Y.
Client: www.motherloadshow.com
Industry: Theater

A Little Soft Shoe

Kids grow up fast—and so do brands, sometimes. That's why Jack and Lily, a Vancouver, B.C.-based soft-sole baby and toddler shoe company, approached Exhibit A: Design Group when they needed a change. "We've actually rebranded this client twice—the first was in 2002," says creative director Cory Ripley. "Our relationship with Jack and Lily began with the design of a simple brochure. Since our initial collaboration, the product line has evolved, so it's only fitting that the brand and its elements continue to adapt as well."

In addition to all aspects of brand development involving the Jack and Lily label, Exhibit A continues to play a leading role in marketing the brand to retail outlets. "The soft-sole baby shoe market has finally matured to accept more than one brand per store," Ripley explains. Positioning Jack and Lily as an alternative against industry leader Robeez and others, Exhibit A "at one point concepted and marketed a Jack and Lily's clothing line to gain acceptance alongside competitors." Eventually, Exhibit A helped move the shoe part of the brand to the forefront.

Inside the retail environment, the Jack and Lily brand has its own distinct image. "The product continues to evolve," Ripley says. "We designed the original line of animal patches [to decorate the shoes] in fur, but later moved to chenille for a more extendable range of color." As a key identifier, they made the brand's signature colors, pink and blue, a little more sophisticated by graying them down slightly. Packaging reflects the Jack and Lily lifestyle image as well, ranging from a transparent, reusable silk-screened bag to a pinstriped display box decorated with silver foil lettering.

Design Firm: Exhibit A: Design Group
Location: Vancouver, B.C., Canada
Client: Jack and Lily
Industry: Baby Shoes

Customers' tactile reaction to the collection, constructed of leather or suede with the exception of the chenille appliqués, gave birth to the Exhibit A penned-slogan, "discover. touch. smile." "Our client's product is softer as a result of the color," explains Ripley. "The more dye added to leather, the stiffer the product." In fact, earlier editions of Jack and Lily shoes featured real lambskin, but they tended to wear thin as small children learned to crawl—something parents didn't smile about when they discovered their children's bare toes touching the living room carpet. "We still refer to the leather as 'lamb touch,' although it's actually cow," says Ripley. "It's one of the softer products on the market and we communicate this as an emotional feature."

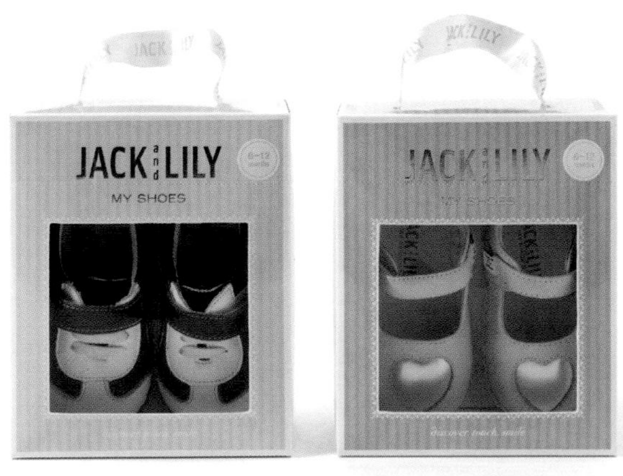

This emotional experience resonates well with the parental market, and as a result, Jack and Lily soft-soled shoes are in demand—and not just for babies and toddlers. "We get asked by friends, family, and customers all the time, 'Can I get these in an adult size?'" Ripley laughs. But soft-soled shoes have certain developmental uses, allowing babies to develop muscles needed for walking. "Our competitors push this benefit, but it's never been a big selling point for us—we focus on the emotional aspects of the experience." Through overall market advertising, though, Ripley feels that the soft-sole advantage has become common knowledge, freeing Jack and Lily to deliver a more straightforward message to this educated market.

Educated *and* style-minded. "We've built the brand around the terms 'soft, fashionable, classic, sophisticated and fun' and use this as our checklist," Ripley says. "We're extremely conscious of this throughout all of our touch points. In [advertisements] we always have something soft in the shot—a plush blanket, or a rug." What about babies? "Not always so soft... They have a window [of attention] of about 10 minutes," Ripley says of photo shoots. "Those Goldfish cracker crumbs get everywhere—they're probably our biggest art direction secret. But please don't tell our competitors."

Design Firm: Kelly Brewster
Location: Charlotte, N.C.
Client: Bella Tunno
Industry: Retail

Design Firm: Bravos Media
Location: Blue Ridge Summit, Penn.
Client: Bellaziza
Industry: Retail

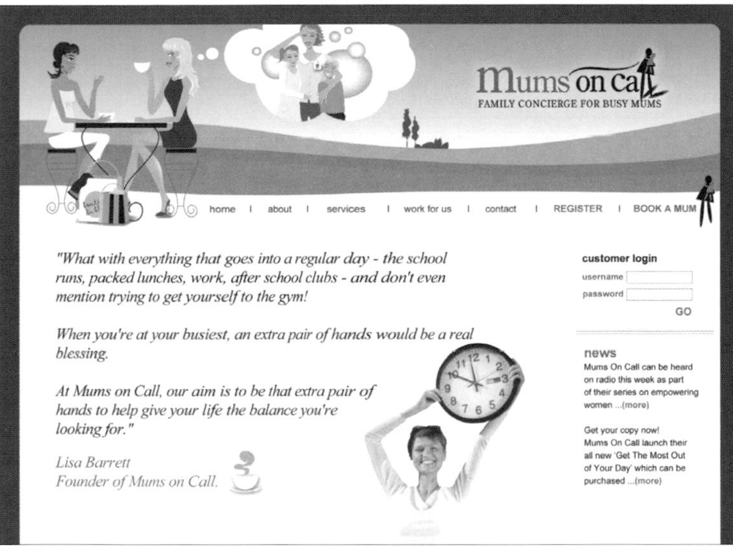

Design Firm: Truly Ace Design
Location: Birmingham, England
Client: Mums on Call
Industry: Childcare

Design Firm: GelComm
Location: Glendale, Calif.
Client: Cranium (Hasbro)
Industry: Toys & Games

Design Firm: GelComm
Location: Glendale, Calif.
Client: Cranium (Hasbro)
Industry: Toys & Games

Serious Play

The owners of children's boutique Peek...Aren't You Curious found their sweet inspiration in a most unexpected way. "Peek found me," says Abbie Planas Gong, founder of San Francisco-based Passing Notes Inc. "They went into Sketch, an ice cream shop I designed."

Gong's whimsy appealed to Peek, who called upon her to infuse pure playfulness into the clothes shopping experience. "Nothing was in place—not even a name," she says. "[Passing Notes] came up with the name, business plan, colors, logos, design and overall branding." The fun starts before you even enter the store—the "peek" theme begins at the front window, where a round clear area suggests a peephole amid a broad expanse of frosted glass and a hand-drawn logo. Even in the parking lot, little hand-drawn characters line the base of the wall—and appear in the most unexpected places later on. "It's playfulness kids can relate to. These little creatures peek in and out of places—like the bottom of a shopping bag or behind a potted plant."

If much of children's art is handmade, Peek's simple décor hides a sophistication that's for the customer to find. Peek's owners came up with the names for their exclusive fashion labels, but Gong gave them life. "They explained the concept of the clothes. Then I came up with a design and color scheme and really made it fun—clothing adults would wear, but for children. The same quality, with thoughtful details and lots of finishing work, elevating it to the same criteria." The whole package is meant to appeal to the discriminating parent and child. "It's iconic American sportswear [evoking] opening day, Lewis and Clark, John Ford," Gong says, referring to Peek's proprietary labels Surf Royalty,

Design Firm: Passing Notes
Location: San Francisco, Calif.
Client: Peek...Aren't You Curious?
Industry: Apparel

SURF
ROYALTY

SURF

CALIFORNIA LIFESTYLE
SURF
royalty

Sgt. Fletcher and Williams and Sons. ("Williams and Sons" refers to the husband of one of the owners and his two sons.)

The family-oriented, fun environment is evident everywhere. "We wanted some playfulness, like instead of racks, we used monkey bars, and put picnic benches in the middle of the store," Gong says. "It's a feeling of warmth familiar to children and adults alike. There's an area for children to read and play with some toys. Each store is different—for example, in the Corte Madera [Calif.] store there's a 10-foot giraffe perched right next to the clothes. There's no way to miss that."

Despite the possible intrusion of a tall African mammal, other touches are more elusive. In addition to the "little creatures" hiding in the parcels and behind furniture, the hide-and-seek motif slips in and out of customers' consciousness with stickers and pinback buttons. "The stickers are a giveaway to children—they love stickers. Also [slogans such as] 'I see you,' 'Made you look' enhance the notion of sight, a peek, a glimpse, a sense of innocence and purity and playfulness." Even the packaging begs to be played with; bags have a hole in them, and instead of boxes, shoppers bring home lidded buckets that parents can use again and again. "At birthday parties, kids want to open the buckets first!" reports Gong proudly.

Inside the store, art turns up everywhere. Gong and Peek collected quotes from such creators as author Shel Silverstein and the painter David Hockney, who noted, "People tend to forget that play is serious." And so is decorating; on the mantle is actual artwork by the founders' children. "As they open more stores, more drawings are being commissioned," Gong says. "Parents are proud of their children's originals—just like their child is an original."

WILLIAMS
AND SONS
extra small
MADE IN CHINA • ONE HUNDRED PERCENT
MACHINE WASH COLD • DO NOT BLEACH

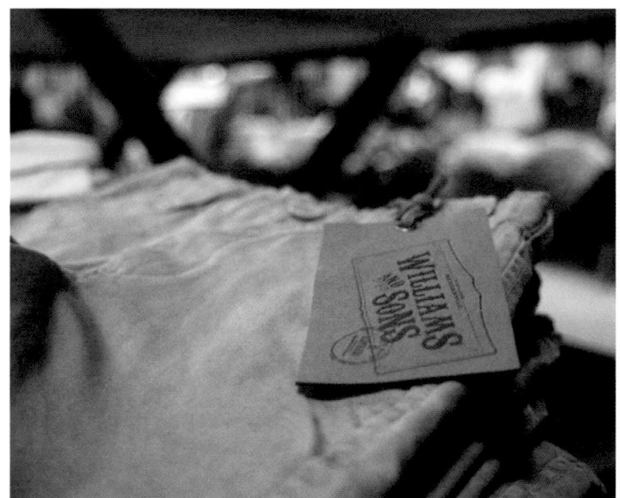
WILLIAMS
AND SONS

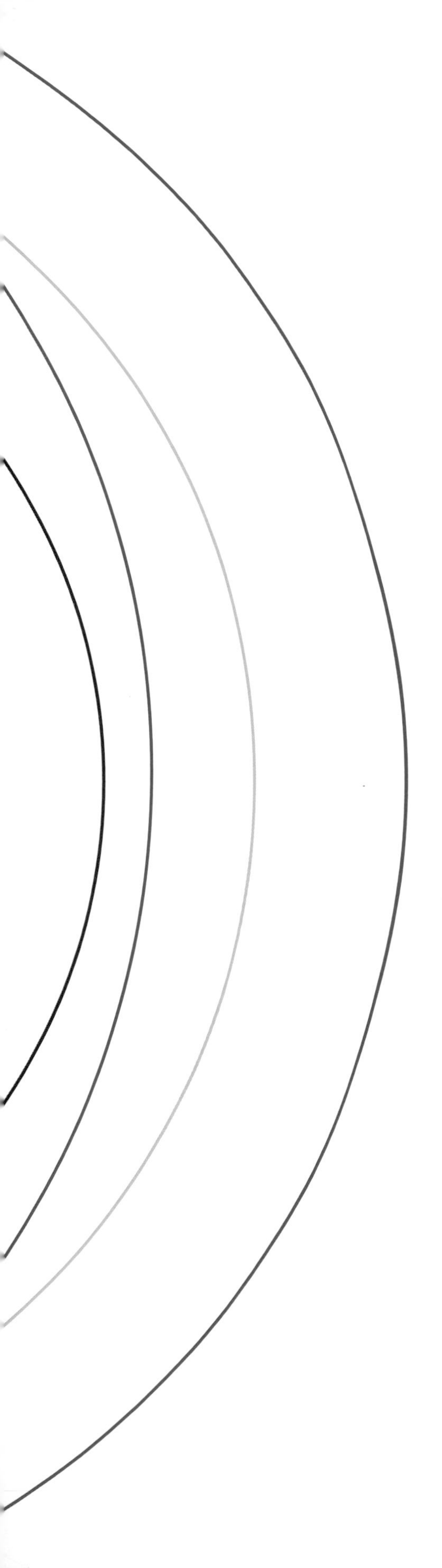

Sports Enthusiasts

OLN and Versus

An aggressive acquisition campaign has largely fueled the growth of Comcast Corporation, the largest cable TV company in the nation and the second-biggest ISP. But after Comcast tried and failed to acquire Disney and its cable sports property ESPN (reaching an estimated 91 million households), Comcast began to retool its own OLN property to expand its reach into the sports market.

Comcast launched OLN (formerly Outdoor Life Network, a nod to the century-old magazine of the same name) in 1997, when it still was known by its original name and its core audience hooked on old-school, outdoorsman-themed programming.

To run with the big dogs, Comcast knew it had to hold onto OLN's existing outdoors types while attracting the archetypal sports junkie. To build a new OLN brand to match its expanded target audience, Comcast turned to the Hollywood-based strategic design consultancy BIRD.

The intention, according to BIRD's creative director Peter King Robbins, was to create something immediately evocative of sports. The result was a "sticker" mark—a slightly rounded rectangle with an inscribed "OLN" reversed in white against an aggressively red field.

According to Robbins, the custom, semi-serifed font in the OLN rebranding recalls the bold, hard-edged type associated with a varsity sports letter, combining thick and thin elements. It is further italicized to raise the energy level and imply motion—or, Robbins explains, to suggest moving *with*.

Design Firm: BIRD
Location: Hollywood, Calif.
Client: Comcast Corporation
Industry: Broadcasting

Robbins rebranded the OLN sticker to look equally at home on the side of an Indy racer, football helmet or tackle box. Says Robbins: "I knew we nailed it when I slapped a prototype on the back of my pickup truck and took a look."

The OLN mark came in different flavors, too: a two-dimensional mark for print and a broadcast version with a three-dimensional energy conveyed by a gray tonal gradation in the lettering and border. BIRD also delivered print and on-air ads along with brand guidelines.

The new look, however, was really just a bridge. Robbins' team at BIRD learned of Comcast's new rebranding of OLN, Versus—a reference to the winner-or-loser nature of competitive games—in early 2006, just six months after the OLN rebranding launch.

The Versus rebranding—launched in the fall of 2006—sustains the equity established in the new OLN logo's type and palette. However, the expanded target audience—hungry for anything involving teams or a stick and a ball—demanded an even higher testosterone level. To this end, BIRD added a hard-core black to the red—raising the energy even more and better implying the dark side of competition—and uniformly thickened the characters.

Along with the Versus wordmark, BIRD designed another sticker logo for the second rebranding. This time, the abbreviated form of VERSUS was set in red type in a black circular field, with the *v* slightly surmounting the *s*. Instead of the tonal gradation of the OLN rebranding's sticker, BIRD gave the VS. logo a metallic look more appropriate for a high-profile television network.

In just a few months, the leafiness of the old Outdoor Life Network had been transformed—twice—from soft and friendly to dangerous and edgy.

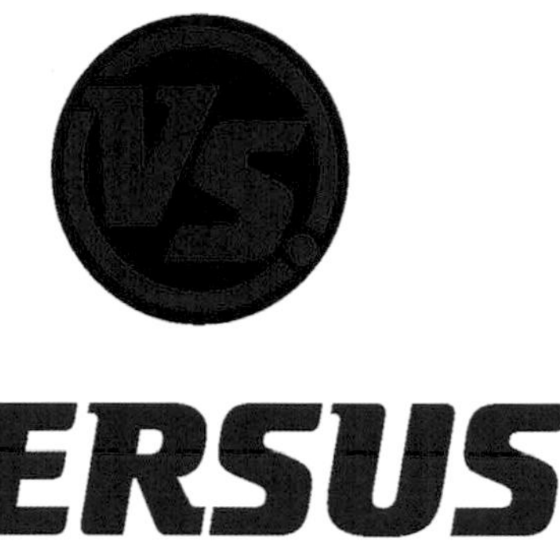

Design Firm: University of South Dakota
Location: Vermillion, S.D.
Client: Various Retailers
Industry: Athletic Apparel

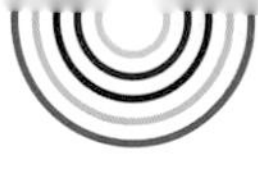

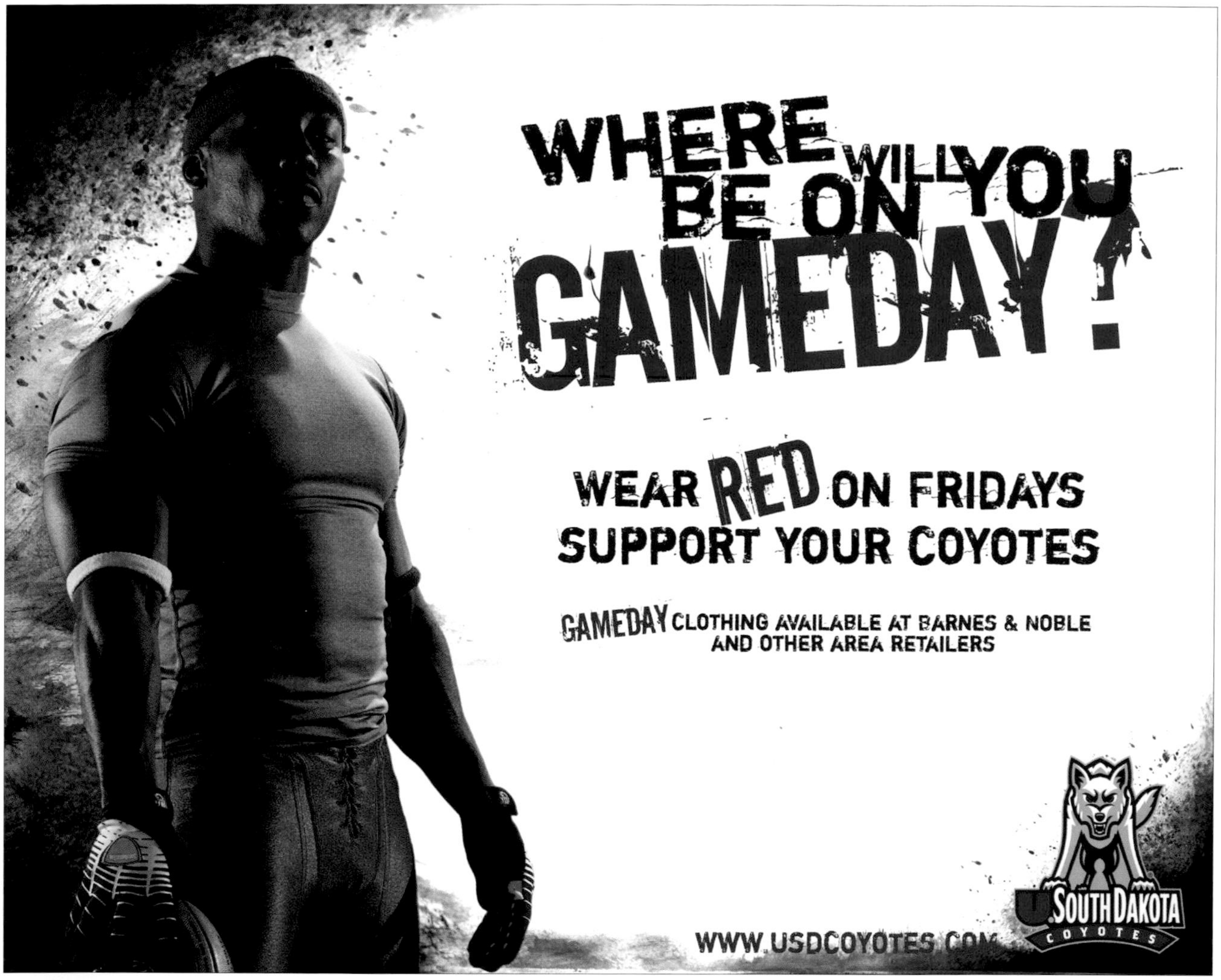
WHERE WILL YOU BE ON GAMEDAY?
WEAR RED ON FRIDAYS
SUPPORT YOUR COYOTES
GAMEDAY CLOTHING AVAILABLE AT BARNES & NOBLE AND OTHER AREA RETAILERS
WWW.USDCOYOTES.COM
SOUTH DAKOTA
COYOTES

WHERE WILL YOU BE ON GAMEDAY?
GAMEDAY MERCHANDISE AVAILABLE HERE
SOUTH DAKOTA
COYOTES

WHERE WILL YOU BE ON GAMEDAY?
SOUTH DAKOTA
SOUTH DAKOTA
COYOTES

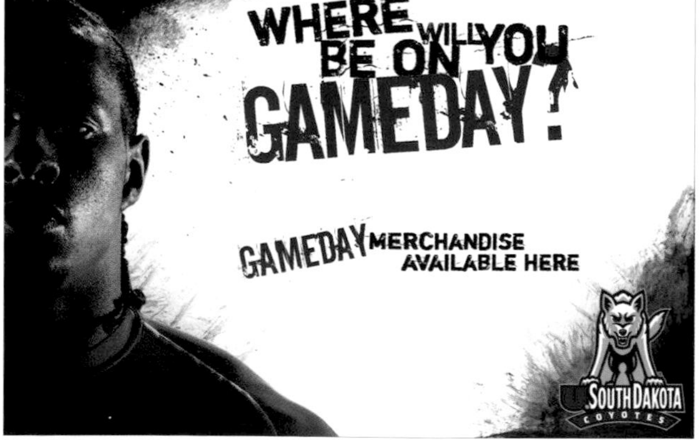

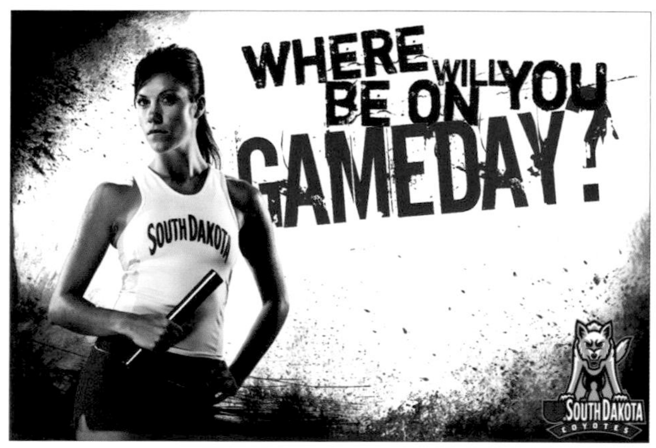

Design Firm: University of South Dakota
Location: Vermillion, S.D.
Client: Various Retailers
Industry: Athletic Apparel

Design Firm: OrangeSeed Design
Location: Minneapolis, Minn.
Client: Twin Cities Marathon Inc.
Industry: Athletic Events

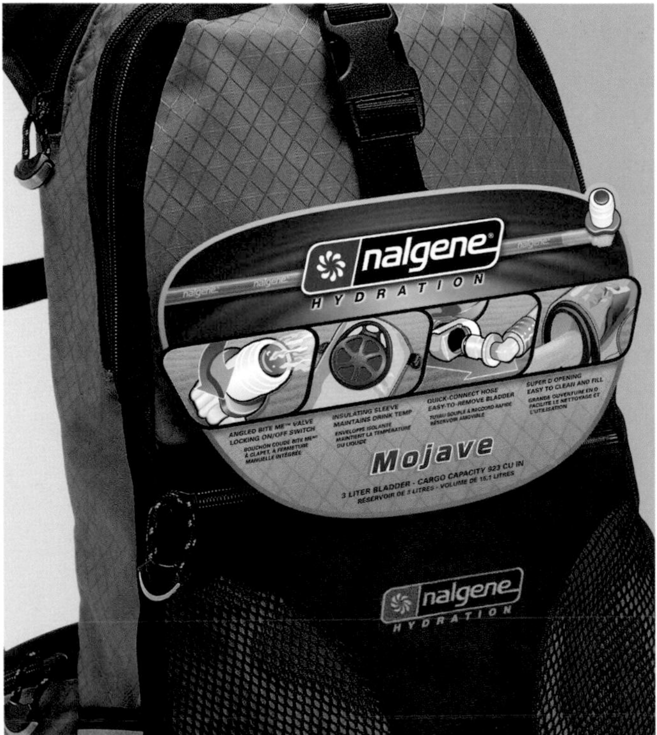

Design Firm: McElveney & Palozzi Design Group
Location: Rochester, N.Y.
Client: Nalgene
Industry: Sporting Goods

Design Firm: Laura Coe Design Associates
Location: San Diego, Calif.
Client: ScubaPro
Industry: Sporting Goods

Design Firm: Siquis
Location: Baltimore, Md.
Client: Dolfin Swimwear
Industry: Sporting Goods

Design Firm: Rotor
Location: Minneapolis, Minn.
Client: Spiderwire/Pure Fishing
Industry: Sporting Goods

Design Firm: JGA
Location: Southfield, Mich.
Client: VF Outdoor Inc.
Industry: Retail

THE
NORTH
FACE

BUILT

JOHN SPRIGGS

FOR A HOSTILE WORLD

JOHN SPRIGGS IS BUILT FOR A HOSTILE WORLD, AND SO IS HIS DNA.

At 19, the 6'5" John Spriggs already casts a huge shadow in the freeskiing world. With ice water in his veins and DNA on his back, Spriggs crushes the competition and makes super human tricks look effortless. As always, you'll only find Spriggs and his DNA shredding at the sickest slopes and at your finest local freeride shop. Check out the full line of DNA winter gear and see what the boys are up to at: RIDEDNA.COM/SPRIGGS

JS

Design Firm: Toolbox Creative
Location: Fort Collins, Colo.
Client: DNA/Descente
Industry: Ski Apparel

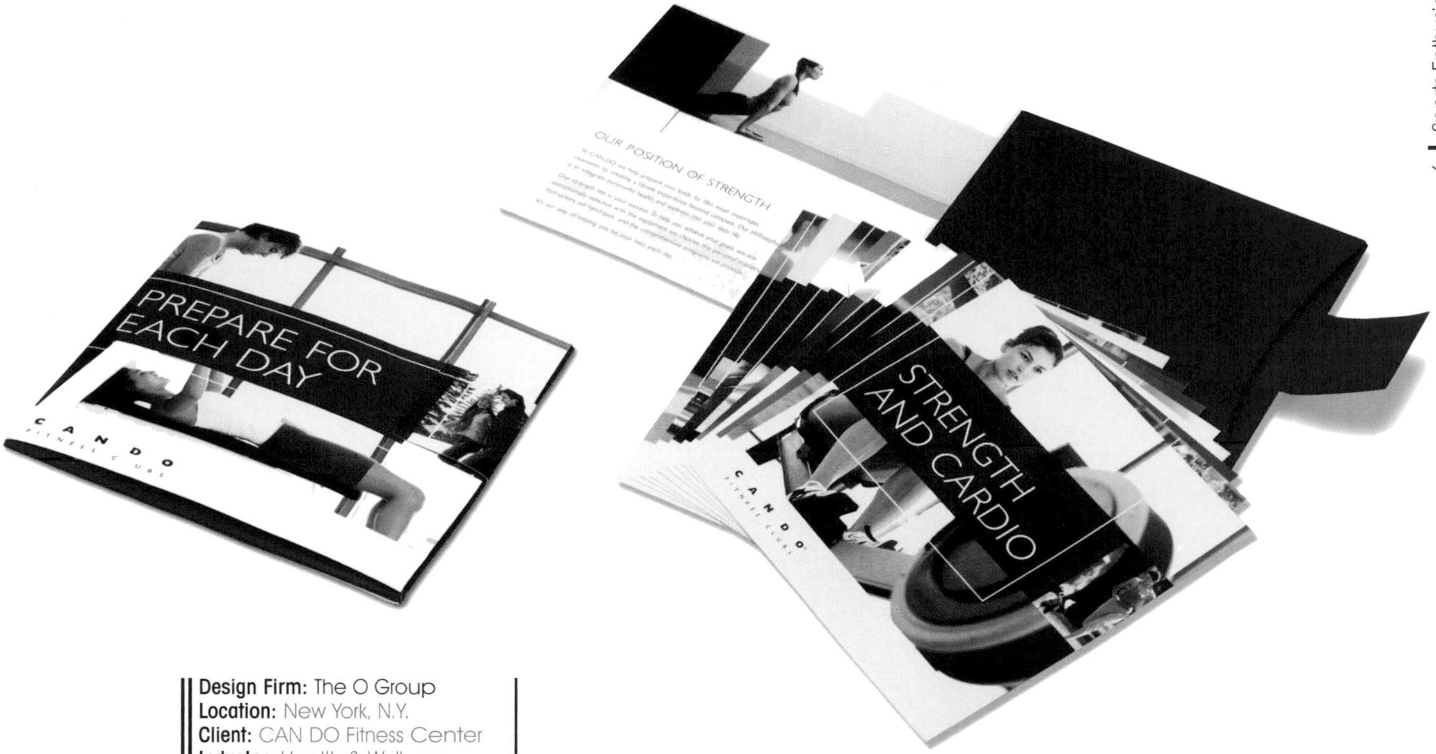

Design Firm: The O Group
Location: New York, N.Y.
Client: CAN DO Fitness Center
Industry: Health & Wellness

Design Firm: Arcanna, Inc.
Location: Peekskill, N.Y.
Client: American Quality Beverages
Industry: Beverage

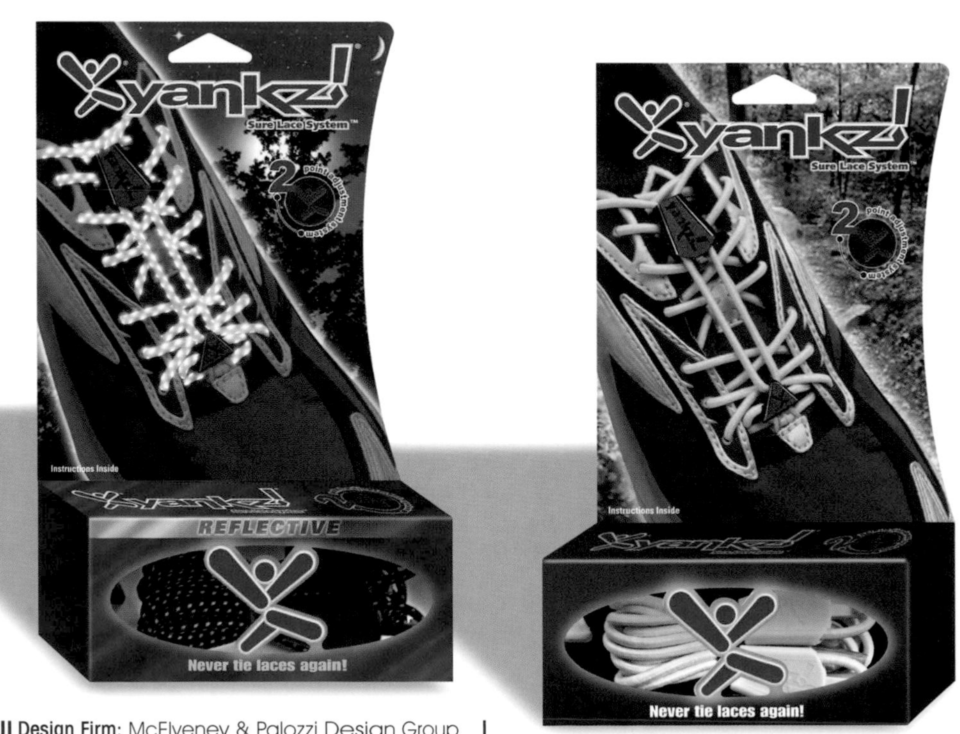

Design Firm: McElveney & Palozzi Design Group
Location: Rochester, N.Y.
Client: Yankz!
Industry: Sporting Goods

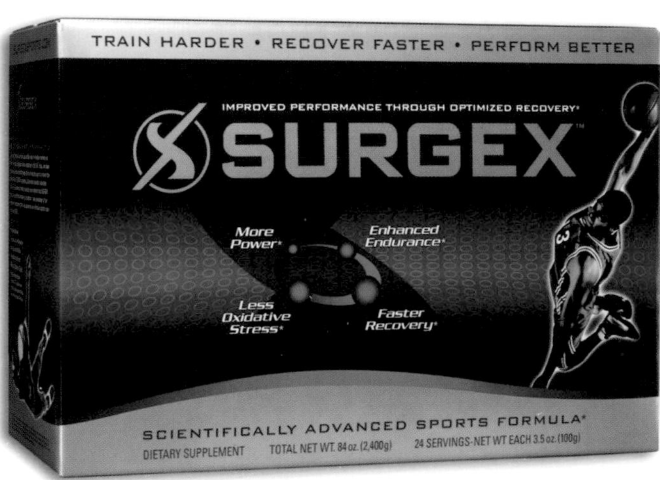

Design Firm: Silver Creative Group
Location: South Norwalk, Conn.
Client: Surgex Sports Inc.
Industry: Sports Nutrition

Design Firm: Miller Meiers Design for Communication
Location: Lawrence, Kan.
Client: Livinity Inc.
Industry: Health & Wellness

Timberland
PRO
PRO SERIES

MEASURE UP
Timberl
PRO SERIE

Design Firm: JGA
Location: Southfield, Mich.
Client: The Timberland Company
Industry: Retail

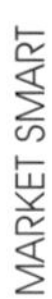

Design Firm: Become/Henrik Persson
Location: Stockholm, Sweden
Client: Sports
Industry: Sporting Goods

Design Firm: Redfixfive
Location: Irvine, Calif.
Client: Giant Bicycles
Industry: Cycling

Design Firm: Watt International
Location: Toronto, Ont., Canada
Client: 3rd Nature
Industry: Retail

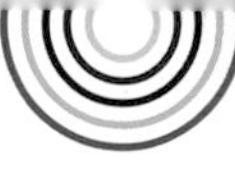

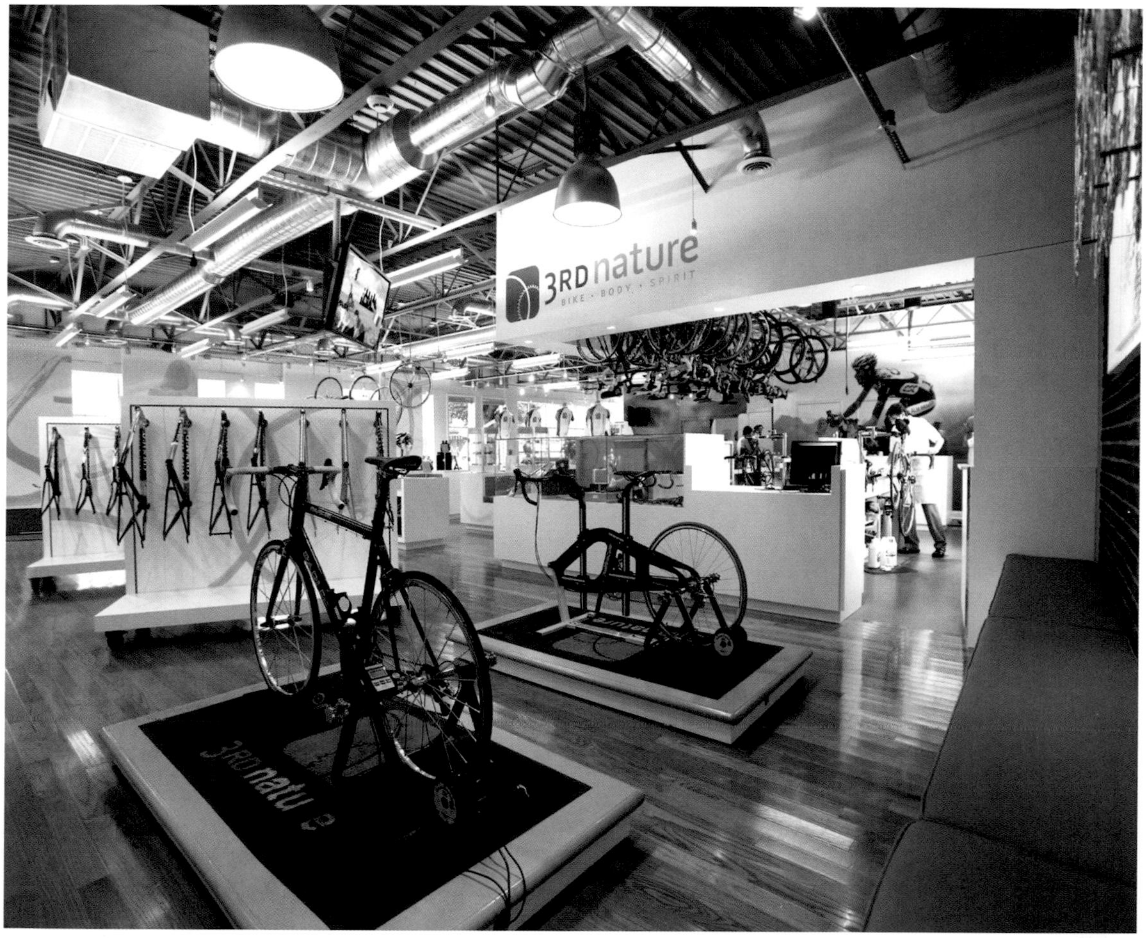
3RD nature
BIKE · BODY · SPIRIT

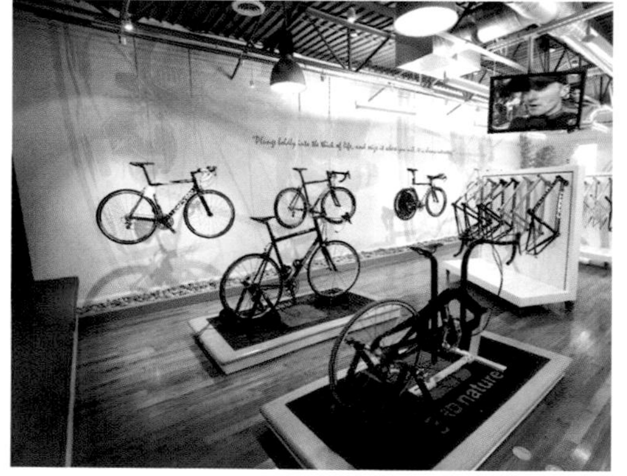

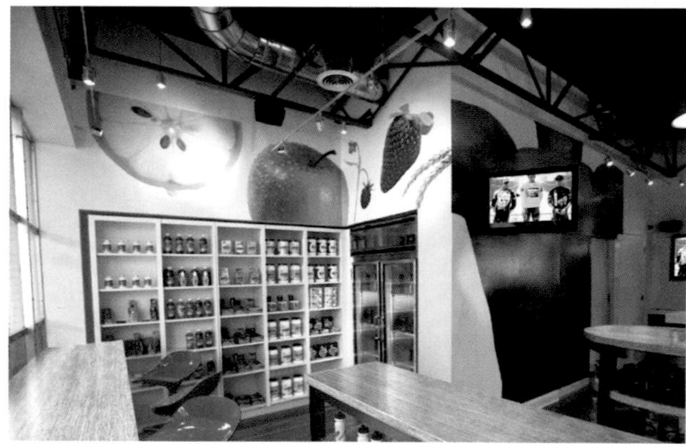

Clubhouse of Brands

Making over a store focused on a sport so firmly entrenched in culture can be a big task. So when Edwin Watts Golf approached Southfield, Mich. agency JGA to turn a golf superstore into a fully accessible shopping experience, JGA drew on both their experience redesigning stores and their wish lists as potential customers themselves.

"It's not only for the avid golfer but an environment that isn't intimidating to the novice," David Nelson, vice president of client strategy, says of Edwin Watts Golf's Concord, N.C. store. "A lot of golf stores look like country clubs, with lots of dark mahogany and hunter green, and that was not where the client wanted to take it."

In giving the customer room to breathe and not feel overwhelmed, JGA spread the merchandise throughout the 9,700-square-foot retail area, allowing lots of room in a store considered small by some standards. "Other stores are two to three times larger," says senior designer Kim Thompson. "We gave it an airy feel. You can see the golf clubs in their entirety; that's a very important part of selecting equipment."

"We wanted to make it a branded house rather than a house of brands," says Nelson. "When the client came to us, they were looking to unify the Edwin Watts brand. Before, it was filled with vendor fixtures without a cohesive look." He notes that companies such as Nike and Callaway pay a lot of money to have their brands featured—but their inclusion doesn't overwhelm the consumer; instead, the focus is *on* the customer.

Design firm: JGA
Location: Southfield, Mich.
Client: Edwin Watts Golf
Industry: Sports Equipment

"When you enter the store, the customer sees three strike points to convey their authority in these areas," says Nelson. "There's the self-serve shoe wall that bridges the men's and women's apparel sections, an equipment array that says that Edwin Watts is *the* authority on golf and the Edwin Watts Golf Academy"—a place where golfers can go to be professionally fitted for the right club by "professional sales associates who can help you improve your game." Even though the area existed in the store's previous incarnation, bringing it front and center served to bring the customer to the forefront as well. The rear of the store features a relaxation area with club chairs and flat-screen monitors streaming sports events. And, according to Nelson, even the art on the wall is for sale. "You can purchase a picture of Jack Nicklaus winning the Masters for your den." One of the goals of the redesign, says Nelson, was to "bring the outside in." The rear wall in the clothing area has a pale green and sunny yellow color palette, and the checkout area features a natural fieldstone wall behind it as a signature element. "The store's colors are those you might expect to see on a golf course," Nelson says. Adds Thompson, "The engineered wood floor and green carpet are integrated to bring together the soft side." And the rubber flooring in the equipment area serves multiple purposes: "If someone wants to try out a club, they're not going to damage the club or the floor," says Nelson. "Plus it's recycled, which is a bonus."

The rubber flooring isn't the only durable feature. According to Nelson, the bay wall dividers are flexible in order to accommodate various brands and seasonal promotions. "It provides flexible fixturing to accommodate changing brands and promotional events," says Thompson.

"We want to make the shopping experience as fun as playing the game," says Nelson. "The environment brings the golfing experience to life."

Design Firm: Siquis
Location: Baltimore, Md.
Client: Dolfin Swimwear
Industry: Sporting Goods

Design Firm: Laura Coe Design Associates
Location: San Diego, Calif.
Client: Trion:Z
Industry: Sporting Goods

Design Firm: Device
Location: London, England
Client: Giro
Industry: Sporting Goods

Design Firm: Version-X Design
Location: Burbank, Calif.
Client: Scratt Surf
Industry: Sporting Goods

Design Firm: Storm Corporate Design
Location: Auckland, New Zealand
Client: Bravo
Industry: Cosmetic and Sports

Design Firm: Levine & Associates Inc.
Location: Washington, D.C.
Client: Verizon Center
Industry: Sports & Entertainment

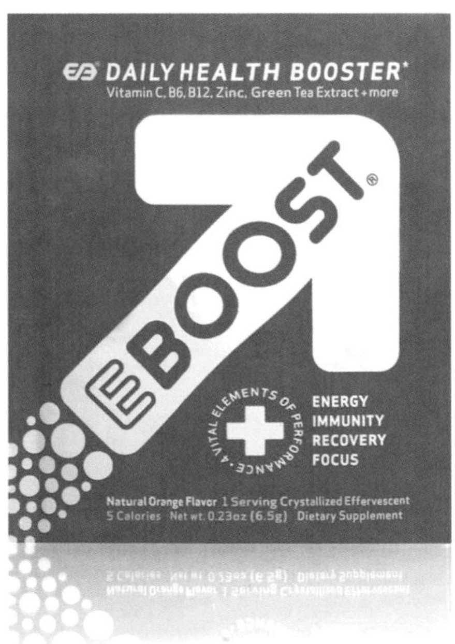

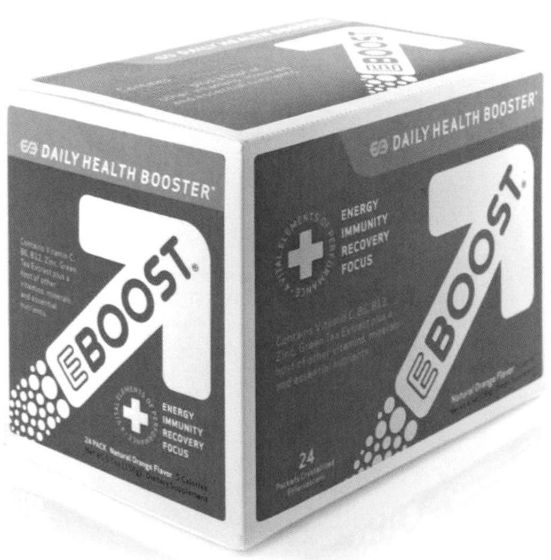

Design Firm: Hana Marie Newman
Location: Brooklyn, N.Y.
Client: EBOOST
Industry: Energy Drink/Vitamin Supplement

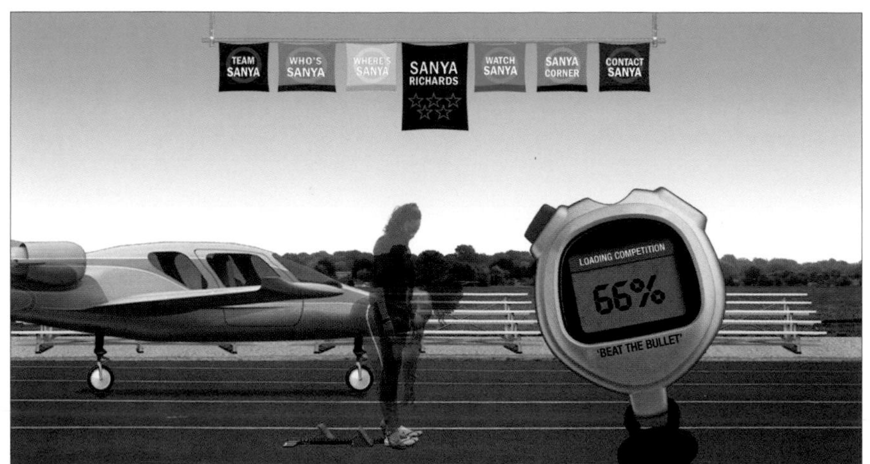

Design Firm: Gigapixel Creative
Location: New York, N.Y.
Client: Sanya Richards
Industry: Self-Promotion

Design Firm: The UXB
Location: Beverly Hills, Calif.
Client: Cleatskins
Industry: Athletic Footwear

Finding Freiheit

Olaf Stein, a longtime bicycle enthusiast in Hamburg, felt that his beloved Focus bike needed a makeover, so the Factor Design founder and designer sent a photo of it to Derby City Werke, current licensors of the Focus brand, with a suggestion. "I wrote the managing director and said that they have a lot of potential and maybe we could work together," he says. "Four months later, the product manager called and invited me to the IFMA [an international bicycle trade show] in Cologne. I convinced them it was time for a new identity."

In addition to designing the logo, which appears on clothing, the catalog, water bottles and the bikes themselves, Stein endeavored to bring a new professionalism to the brand. "The product manager is a former pro cyclist," he says. "[Three-time world champion racer] Mike Kluge was a consultant—I said I'd put him more in the front. He won a lot of major races, so I put the product manager, Mike Kluge and another pro rider in the catalog as models." This name and face recognition helped showcase the pros' association with Focus—and the striking graphics Stein designed for the bicycles and everything that goes with them.

The logo itself is a pair of joined letter *f*'s, and on the bicycles it appears on the steering column and at the front and rear of the frame. Says Stein: "I introduced the black and red to differentiate the brand from the competition." (Focus is a popular brand for cyclo-cross racing both in Europe and in the States.

Design Firm: Factor Design
Location: Hamburg, Germany
Client: Focus
Industry: Bicycles

Cyclo-cross is a form of racing that features slightly wider tires than conventional racing bikes, with competitions typically held during the fall and winter months.) "I convinced them that, as a sponsor of professional and semi-professional racing teams, they needed a very simple and strong color code, especially for clothing."

Focus' slogan, "Discover Freedom," is an old one, but one that Stein believes still has relevance for designers and sports enthusiasts. "One problem [for designers] is that there are few bicycle companies around; the major cycling brands in the U.S. aren't the same in Germany," he says. "Sports are attractive for designers but difficult to get a foot in the door." The designs must also be compelling in order to capture the imagination of thebicyclist seeking that same liberating distinction: "You have to stick out. That's what we achieved—because of the black and red jerseys."

7 Foodies

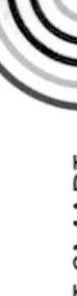

Flight of Fancy

When New Hampshire-based startup Portsmouth Tea Company set out to introduce tea to a new audience, its founder, Marshall Malone, turned to Hans Anderson of HVANDERSON DESIGN—a year after the two met on an airplane. Anderson parlayed his own love of tea into a brand identity unlike any other seen before.

One particular challenge lay in the image of the beverage itself. "There's the Pacific Rim image of tea that it's supposed to bring the drinker into a certain stasis," says Anderson, "and there's the Victorian idea that's staid, prim and proper. We wanted vivacity, humor, a glint in the eye." To this end, Anderson developed a wordmark based on the Bickham typeface, embellished with leaves. "It's an allusion to the product, a very fine grade loose tea. Pacific Rim tends to use a more minimalist text, but we're not afraid of occasional ornamentation. It's got more attitude." This "attitude" works in tandem with a recurring motif throughout the brand: a gentle French curve. "It harmonizes with the mood, historical references, focus," he says, "and it isn't afraid for beauty to be feminine."

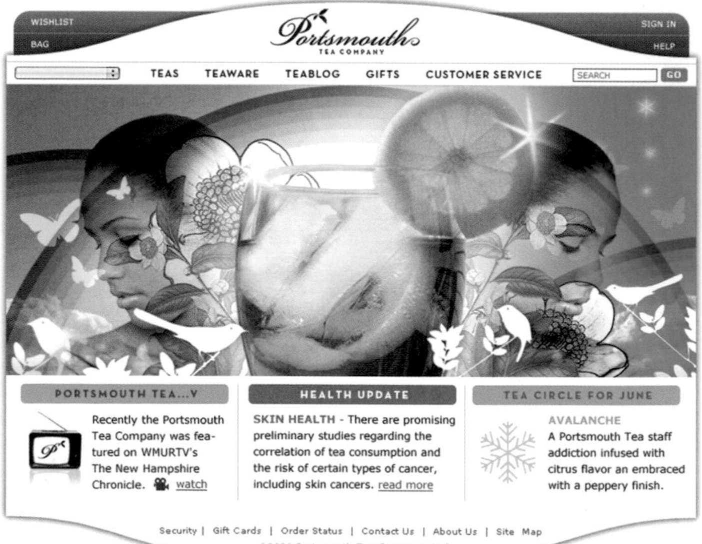

The celebration of the feminine is the undertow that runs rapid beneath the placid image of the world's favorite beverage. Anderson envisioned a sophisticated woman as a consumer—and yet one who is thoroughly accessible. "Imagine an elegant tea café—European with a touch of the exotic," he says, referring again to the design elements' heritage. "It's a little aspirational for an American woman. [When enjoying tea] you get a beautiful, exotic experience. The [American] woman is not Petrarch's Laura on a pedestal, but a very real and approachable woman." The packaging itself is indeed exotic yet approachable.

Design Firm: HVANDERSON DESIGN
Location: Louisville, Ky.
Client: Portsmouth Tea Co.
Industry: Tea

Portsmouth
TEA COMPANY™

The round tins evoke a softness different from its boxy forebears, what Anderson calls "fusty" Victorian and Colonial British imagery. The label itself extends beyond the lid line along that same French curve. "The shape of the label extends that balance we'd love to achieve—between voluptuous beauty but in strict control. There's a real simplicity in conjunction with this." The curve appears yet again in the die-cut shape of the company's business cards; Anderson says it's not unusual for Malone to receive calls simply because would-be clients are impressed with the elegance of his brand's identity.

"People react to a full identity," he continues. "We want Portsmouth to be a very real, very rich personality, but one with certain hallmarks." Along with the French curve, leaves, birds and modified Bickham typeface, an evocative hand-drawn swirl rises from much of the tea depicted in ads and on the Web site. It's a bold move—and it works. "Vapor! Flavor! Life! Spirit! Vivacity!" says Anderson. "Things lacking in the Pacific Rim and Victorian images of tea."

A lovely shape deserves a tasteful cover, which is why Anderson developed "tea" shirts for Portsmouth—many of which feature birds. "Metaphorically, birds are, in history and across cultures and literature, feminine, exuberant, joyful, melodious, curvaceous, free. The bird image gives expression to values that many women share. Plus, they're a fun way to express the brand.... A company is a personality, and Portsmouth means to celebrate freedom of spirit... it could become a lifestyle brand [to appeal to] sensitive people from all walks of life. Tea is really just beginning to take off in the U.S., but there's a longer history with great potential and variety of flavors and a potential to be bigger than coffee."

Design Firm: A Blue Moon Arts LLC
Location: Tulsa, Okla.
Client: Spritz
Industry: Beverage

Design Firm: Parker Williams Design Limited
Location: London, England
Client: Sainsbury's
Industry: Gourmet Chocolate

Design Firm: Parker Williams Design Limited
Location: London, England
Client: Theatre Box
Industry: Gourmet Chocolate

Design Firm: Parker Williams Design Limited
Location: London, England
Client: Llanllyr Water
Industry: Beverage

Design Firm: The O Group
Location: New York, N.Y.
Client: 86 Recipes
Industry: Food & Travel

Design Firm: MiresBall
Location: San Diego, Calif.
Client: Bochner Chocolates
Industry: Gourmet Chocolate

Design Firm: biz-R
Location: Totnes, Devon, England
Client: Heron Valley Organic
Industry: Organic Food Producer

Design Firm: espluga+associates
Location: Barcelona, Spain
Client: Seis Grados/Damm
Industry: Beverages

GODIVA
Chocolatier
CHOCOlixir

Design Firm: JGA
Location: Southfield, Mich.
Client: Godiva Chocolatier
Industry: Retail

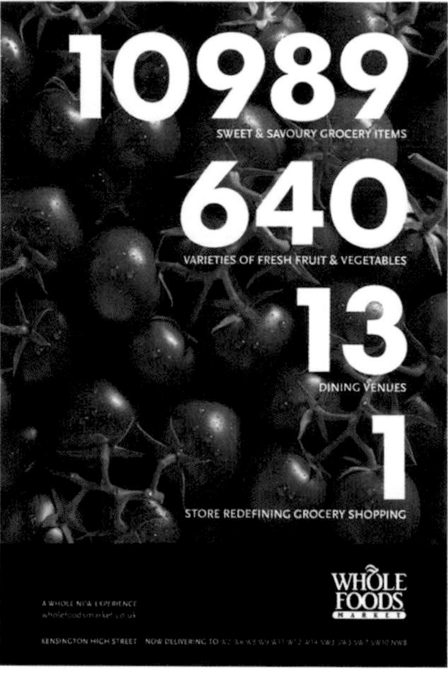

Design Firm: DEEP
Location: London, England
Client: Whole Foods
Industry: Food, Retail

Design Firm: Lolight Design
Location: Austin, Texas
Client: Ann Marie Douglas—Annie's Kitchen
Industry: Catering

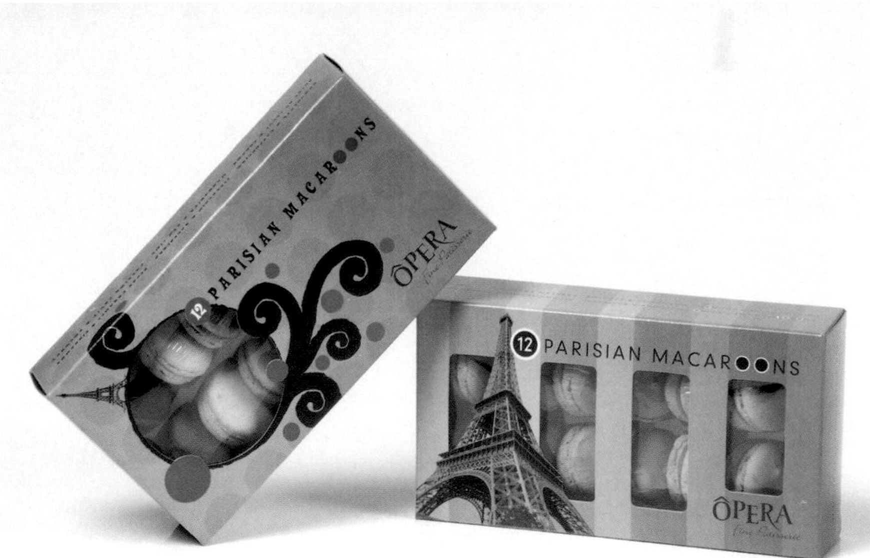

Design Firm: ideaworks advertising
Location: Carlsbad, Calif.
Client: Opera Patisseries
Industry: Food & Beverage

Design Firm: JGA
Location: Southfield, Mich.
Client: Lindt & Spungli
Industry: Retail

Design Firm: FAI Design Group
Location: Irvington, N.Y.
Client: New Jersey Ironmen/Newark Arena
Industry: Food

Design Firm: Philippe Becker
Location: San Francisco, Calif.
Client: Williams-Sonoma
Industry: Food & Beverage

Design Firm: Philippe Becker
Location: San Francisco, Calif.
Client: Cost Plus
Industry: Food & Beverage

Design Firm: Rotor
Location: Minneapolis, Minn.
Client: Community Design Center of Minnesota
Industry: Nonprofit

Design Firm: Rotor
Location: Minneapolis, Minn.
Client: Cooks of Crocus Hill
Industry: Food & Beverage

Design Firm: Philippe Becker
Location: San Francisco, Calif.
Client: Williams-Sonoma
Industry: Food & Beverage

Design Firm: Design Source Creative Inc.
Location: Aptos, Calif.
Client: Mugnaini Imports Inc.
Industry: Food

Design Firm: espluga+associates
Location: Barcelona, Spain
Client: Miguel Torres
Industry: Food

Design Firm: JGA
Location: Southfield, Mich.
Client: Rocky Mountain Chocolate Factory
Industry: Retail

Design Firm: The People's Design
Location: Glendale, Calif.
Client: Ococoa Chocolates
Industry: Food & Beverage

Design firm: WAX
Location: Calgary, Alb., Canada
Client: Calgary Farmers' Market
Industry: Food & Beverage

FRI & SAT 9-5 SUN 9-4 ★ CROWCHILD TR & FLANDERS AVE SW ★ CALGARYFARMERSMARKET.CA **FRESH ALL WINTER**

CALGARY FARMERS' MARKET

Design Firm: yellobee studio
Location: Atlanta, Ga.
Client: Via Elsa
Industry: Food

Design Firm: Parker Williams
Location: London, England
Client: Infuzions
Industry: Food & Beverage

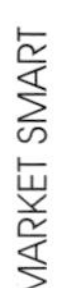

Design Firm: Mark Oliver Inc.
Location: Solvang, Calif.
Client: Honest Foods
Industry: Food & Beverage

Design Firm: John Barnes & Company Inc.
Location: Chicago, Ill.
Client: Georgia Nut Company
Industry: Food & Beverage

Downloads: Reports, Research, Docs

SPREAD

The USAID Agribusiness Project

RWANDA EXPORTS

SPREAD PROJECT

FARMER PORTAL

Nestled among the thousand hills of our remote, tiny African country...

are our farmers.

» LAUNCH PORTAL

FEATURED STORY

The Coffee Bike

is improving the quality of Rwandan Coffee & the livelihood of Rwandan Farmers.

» READ STORY

SPREAD PROJECT

SPREAD works to strengthen the agribusiness process, resulting in exceptional products & improved livelihoods for the Rwandan farmer.

» SPREAD PROJECT

COFFEE WASHING VIDEO

From 1 washing station to over 100 in 4 years, Rwanda has refined its coffee washing process...

» WATCH VIDEO

RWANDA COFFEE

Rwanda's extraordinary specialty coffee has recently become a favorite for distinguished coffee connoisseurs.

» RWANDAN COFFEE

OUR PARTNERS

OCIR Café

USAID

TEXAS A&M AGRICULTURE

» ALL PARTNERS

CUP OF EXCELLENCE

GOING ORGANIC

QUALITY FIRST

FAIR TRADE

BUY RWANDAN COFFEE

GO ON A COFFEE SAFARI

Rwanda's bourban qualifies in preliminary cup of excellence competion.........

This project is funded by USAID - From the American People
Norman Borlaug Institute for International Agriculture

Website designed by IDENTITY AFRICA

Design Firm: IDENTITY AFRICA Advertising Agency
Location: Kigali, Rwanda
Client: SPREAD Project
Industry: Specialty Coffee

Design Firm: Mark Oliver Inc.
Location: Solvang, Calif.
Client: Bellwether Farms
Industry: Dairy

Design Firm: brandUNITY Inc.
Location: Rollingbay, Wash.
Client: Mora Ice Cream
Industry: Food & Beverage

Design Firm: McElveney & Palozzi Design Group
Location: Rochester, N.Y.
Client: Heron Hill Winery
Industry: Beverage

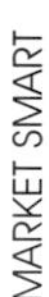

Design Firm: Velocity
Location: Boston, Mass.
Client: Prairie Orchard Farms
Industry: Food & Beverage

Design Firm: Rotor
Location: Minneapolis, Minn.
Client: Cooks of Crocus Hill
Industry: Food & Beverage

Pot of Goodness

You are what you eat—or, in the case of the rebranding of Clive's Organic Bakery, you *see* what you eat. That's the idea behind the packaging of the company's products, available in health food stores across Britain and in select regional groceries.

What's inside is good and good looking. "We didn't want a terrible photograph of a pie cut in half," says Blair Thomson of biz-R, the Devon design firm. "The Mexican chili pie sleeve uses bold imagery of big bright chilies as the background," he cites as one example. "Pie is encased in pastry so you can't see what's inside, so for these products we have boldly focused on the predominant ingredient."

The agency used colors and clean typography to refresh the brand—which includes pies, flapjacks, pastry, gluten-free pies and cakes and freshly prepared "Pot of" meals, inspired by culinary traditions of the world—along with a simple, WYSIWYG approach to the packaging of the entire product range.

The "Pot of" line features an international flavor in more ways than one, without the frills—or the pastry. "By using 'Pot of' as the name, we have formed a description of the actual product—a 'pot of' Moroccan tagine, Thai curry or aduki bean stew," he says. "Some people don't want to eat pastries, so Clive's developed this alternative which can be eaten as is, or used in recipes."

With the product being so visible the 'Pot of' sleeve doesn't need to show explicitly what's in the package. "We took the whole front section out and left the sleeve with about one-third of the pot to view. We wanted customers to see what's inside, therefore we didn't need to use any photo on the sleeve," he says; with the transparent container, "you can see what you will eat."

Design Firm: biz-R
Location: Totnes, Devon, England
Client: Clive's Organic Bakery
Industry: Organic Food & Beverage

Clive's
made with love

To illustrate each product's particular cultural heritage on the outside, "We used a distinctive, bold, graphic approach that's quite distinctively reflective of each recipe's country of origin," Thomson says. "A Moroccan [entrée] uses Moroccan symbology, Thai uses Thai symbology." While the "Pot of" packages sit comfortably within the Clive's product range, with their VAG Rounded typography and similar coloring, close examination reveals culturally significant symbols and color to differentiate each recipe. "Aduki is a Chinese bean, but here it has been used in an English spring vegetable stew," he says. "So, we used a Chinese symbol, which also lends itself to English gardens and such."

Speaking of gardens, Clive's tagline, "Made with love," reflects the homegrown ethos of the brand, and biz-R adapted the slogan so it became a part of the logo. "Clive's literally make all the products by hand—they put a lot of love into it!" says Thomson. "Every single place where you see handwriting [such as the word *organic*] is unique—real handwriting—so we put our own hand-made stamp on it. It makes the packaging reflective of the quality of the product and it encapsulates the essence of home cooking."

Healthy home cooking, that is. "The 'Pot of' recipes claim to contain up to four of your five recommended daily vegetable servings in each pot," Thomson says. "Have a fruit juice as well and that's all of it." But there's more to it than eating greens for the sake of trendiness: "Vegetarian [products] had, for a long time, been more of an alternative health food option, with a hippie image," he explains. "One of the key objectives of the Clive's rebrand was that they wanted to appeal to a wider, not necessarily vegetarian, market, a more brand-aware consumer who is interested in food and a healthy lifestyle."

The biz-R crew are fans of the products as well, particularly the "Pot of" line. "We eat them all the time! Only half of our staff is vegetarian but they're a healthy option—so many [other prepackaged entrées] are so high in fat and high in calories," Thomson says. "These contain no genetically modified ingredients, and most are vegan as well." Thomson and the biz-R team know that they're eating something special, because they helped make it so. "Differentiation is the key to the success of this rebrand," he says.

Notes

1 C&R Research, *Holiday Wish List and Habits Survey*, Winter 2008

2 James McNeil quoted in Horovitz, B. (2006, November 22). *Six Strategies Marketers use to Make Kids Want Things Bad. USA Today*, p. 1B and Schor, J. (2004). *Born to Buy: The Commercialized Child and the New Consumer Culture*. New York: Scribner

3 James McNeal quoted in *BuyBabies*. (2006, December 9). *The Economist and Schor*, J. (2004) *Born to Buy: The Commercialized Child and the New Consumer Culture*. New York: Scribner

4 Yankelovich, Inc., *Youth MONITOR* 2003

5 Yankelovich, Inc., *Youth MONITOR* 2005

6 Ann Hulbert, "Tweens 'R' Us," *The New York Times*, November 28, 2004

7 Donald F. Roberts, Ulla G. Foehr, Victoria Rideout, *Generation M: Media in the Lives of 8-18 Year-Olds*, The Henry J. Kaiser Family Foundation, March 9, 2005

8 Siegel, David L., Timothy J. Coffey, Gregory Livingston (2004). *The Great Tween Buying Machine*. New York: Kaplan Business

9 Forrester Research, "Young Consumers And Technology" (2005)

10 American Express, "Third Annual American Express Platinum Luxury Survey" (2006)

11 New Strategist Publications, 2003 and Reynolds, Christopher (2004, May 1). *Overlooked & Under X-Ploited, American Demographics*

12 C&R Research, "Boomer Heartbeat"

13 American Express, "Third Annual American Express Platinum Luxury Survey" (2006) and J. Walter Thompson

14 Reynolds, Christopher (2004, May 1). *Overlooked & Under X-Ploited, American Demographics*

15 Reynolds, Christopher (2004, May 1). *Overlooked & Under X-Ploited, American Demographics*

16 C&R Research, "Heartbeat," The Boomer Project and GetInvolved.gov.

17 Emarketer, "Baby Boomers and Silver Surfers: Two Generations Online" (December 2007)

18 J. Walker Smith, president of Yankelovich Partners, quoted in Adler, Jerry, et.al. (November 14, 2005). *The Boomer Files Newsweek*

19 AARP, "It's Good to be Green: Socially Conscious Shopping Behaviors Among Boomers," 2007

20 The Boomer Project

INDEX